Jane Bull
Crafty Creatures

DK

LONDON, NEW YORK, MUNICH,
MELBOURNE, and DELHI

DESIGN AND TEXT Jane Bull
PHOTOGRAPHER Andy Crawford
SENIOR EDITOR Carrie Love
US SENIOR EDITOR Shannon Beatty
US EDITOR Margaret Parrish
DESIGNER Hannah Moore
PRODUCTION EDITOR Raymond Williams
PRODUCTION CONTROLLER Ché Creasey
CREATIVE DIRECTOR Jane Bull
CATEGORY PUBLISHER Mary Ling

First American Edition, 2013
Published in the United States by DK Publishing
4th floor, 345 Hudson Street
New York, New York 10014

13 14 15 16 17   10 9 8 7 6 5 4 3 2 1
001–185426–09/13
Copyright © 2013 Dorling Kindersley Limited
Copyright © 2013 Jane Bull
All rights reserved.

A catalog record for this book
is available from the Library of Congress.
ISBN: 978-1-4654-0914-0

DK books are available at special discounts when
purchased in bulk for sales promotions, premiums,
fund-raising, or educational use. For details, contact:
DK Publishing Special Markets, 345 Hudson Street,
New York, New York 10014 or SpecialSales@dk.com.

Printed and bound in China
by South China Printing Co. Ltd.

Discover more at
www.dk.com

Meet the creatures

Creature craft

Meet a host of animal characters

The projects in this book are all simple to make—
they're good for beginners and experienced crafters
alike. All you need to get started is a basic grasp of
sewing and knitting, plus the essential sewing kit.
The materials required for each craft are listed at
the start of each project. Happy making!

Sewing kit

Page 112

1

Woolly animals

Yarn octopus

This crazy octopus is great for practicing your braiding skills and for using up leftover yarn. For a different look, create a multicolored creature.

You will need
- 1 x ball brightly colored DK yarn • 12in (30cm) piece thick cardboard • 1 x ball scrunched-up foil
- Googly eyes • Scissors

Make the foil ball slightly smaller than a tennis ball.

Fashion a pretty bow tie for your octopus out of ribbon.

How to make lots of legs

1

Wind the yarn around the cardboard about 40 times.

Secure the yarn end to the cardboard.

2

Place a piece of yarn under the wound yarn at the top and tie it together firmly.

Cut through the bundle of yarn.

3

Lay the center of the bundle over the ball.

4

Spread the strands of yarn evenly over the ball.

Hold the ball firmly and tie a piece of yarn under the ball.

Divide each bunch into three equal sections.

5

Divide the bundle into eight equal bunches.

Secure the braid with a piece of yarn tied in a bow.

Braid each leg.

Knittens

To make a knitted kitten, knit striped shapes, sew them together, and stuff with poly fill until your little kitty is soft and cuddly. Add button eyes, and you have a knitten!

You will need
- Solid-colored DK-weight yarn for body and contrasting colors for clothes
- Size 6 (4mm) knitting needles
- Tapestry needle • Poly fill
- Buttons for eyes
- Sewing kit (page 112)

Head

Top
Sleeve

Paws

Pants
Feet

Begin knitting from the feet upward.

How to knit a knitten

To make the knitten's body

Cast on 34 stitches in brown yarn.
Work in stockinette stitch (page 121),
Feet: Starting with a row of knit stitch,
work 4 rows.
Pants: Change yarn color (page 116)
and work 13 rows.
Top: Change yarn color and
work 10 rows.
Head: Change yarn color and work
16 rows.
Cast off.

To make the arms

Cast on 9 stitches in brown yarn.
Work in stockinette stitch.
Paws: Starting with a row of
knit stitch, work 4 rows.
Sleeve: Change yarn color
and make 10 rows.
Cast off.

Knitten know-how

The secret to the knitten's shape is in the finishing. Sew the two long sides together and turn the material the right way out, making sure the seam is at the center back. This will be where the legs are shaped.

Stripes or solids?

Stripes are pretty, but the knitten's top will look just as nice in a solid color, and it will be simpler to make, too. Easier still—if you use variegated yarn you'll get a colorful effect automatically.

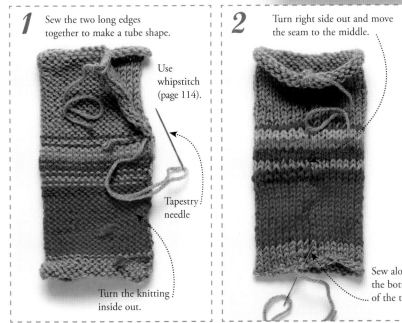

1 Sew the two long edges together to make a tube shape.
Use whipstitch (page 114).
Tapestry needle
Turn the knitting inside out.

2 Turn right side out and move the seam to the middle.
Sew along the bottom of the tube.

3 Fill the knitted tube, but not too full.
Sew along the edge to close the opening.

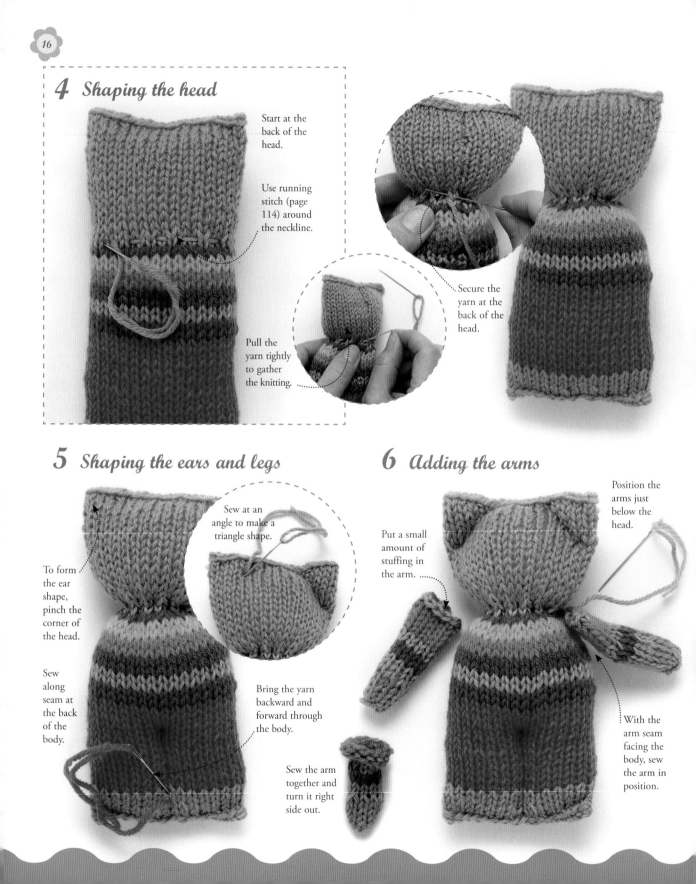

4 Shaping the head

Start at the back of the head.

Use running stitch (page 114) around the neckline.

Pull the yarn tightly to gather the knitting.

Secure the yarn at the back of the head.

5 Shaping the ears and legs

Sew at an angle to make a triangle shape.

To form the ear shape, pinch the corner of the head.

Sew along seam at the back of the body.

Bring the yarn backward and forward through the body.

Sew the arm together and turn it right side out.

6 Adding the arms

Position the arms just below the head.

Put a small amount of stuffing in the arm.

With the arm seam facing the body, sew the arm in position.

Cats and kittens

Cats come in all shapes and sizes. It's possible to make big and little cats by knitting different-sized rectangles. Cast on more stitches for fat cats or knit more stripes for long and lean cats.

Add buttons for eyes.

Tops and pants

The bands of knitted stripes will become the knitten's body parts. The tops can be solid, or you can dress your knitten in striped sweaters, like those shown here.

Large-sized knitten

Variegated

Use variegated yarn to create a multicolored sweater without having to change yarns.

Baby-sized knitten

18

Hey,
Koala Kid!
Introduce me to your friends.

Koala   Koala Kid   Gray Bear   Mouse   Knitten

Koala Bear and friends

It's all about the ears—that's what makes these critters different. Knit the body as you would for a knitten, then knit rounded or pointed ear shapes to create other creatures.

Big Knitten

The Rabbits and Polar Bear

Raccoon

How to knit koalas...

These koalas are made in the same way as the knittens on page 14. Knit rectangular shapes for the arms and body, making stripes to form the head, body, and paws. The rounded ears look just like a koala's.

To make a round head, shape the knitting at the top.

The neck has been gathered on this stripe to turn his sweater into a turtleneck.

Koala Kid

FOR BODY
Cast on 24 stitches.
Work in stockinette stitch.
Legs: 10 rows.
Body: 18 rows.
Head: 15 rows.

FOR ARMS
Cast on 8 stitches.
Work in stockinette stitch.
Paws: 4 rows.
Arms: 12 rows.

FOR EARS
Cast on 8 stitches.
Work 5 rows in stockinette stitch.
Attach ears as shown on the next page.

Koala Bear

FOR BODY
Cast on 48 stitches.
Work in stockinette stitch.
Legs: 20 rows.
Body: 36 rows.
Head 30 rows.

FOR ARMS
Cast on 16 stitches.
Work in stockinette stitch.
Paws: 8 rows.
Arms 24 rows.

FOR EARS
Cast on 16 stitches.
Work 10 rows in stockinette stitch.
Attach as shown opposite.

... and friends

The Rabbits
Ears: Cast on 6.
Work 14 rows.

Raccoon
Ears: Cast on 4.
Work 5 rows.

Mouse
See opposite.

Polar Bear
Ears: Cast on 4.
Work 5 rows.
Work in stripes as for Koala.

Gray Bear
Ears: Cast on 6.
Work 6 rows.

Work in multicolored stripes. Work as for Koala.

Legs: Work 11 rows. Body: Work 14 rows. Head: Work 15 rows. Arms: 12 rows for arm, 4 rows for sleeve.

Legs: Work 6 rows. Body: Work 10 rows for pants, 8 rows for top. Head: Work 15 rows. Work arms as for Koala.

Legs: Work 6 rows. Body: Work 18 rows (work in two colored stripes). Head: Work 8 rows gray yarn, 3 rows black yarn, 5 rows gray yarn. Work arms as for Koala.

Making faces

Place a disk of white fabric on the reverse side of the face. Sew the features in place.

MOUSE
Ears: Cast on 6.
Work 6 rows.

Legs: 6 rows.
Body: 11 rows for pants, 9 rows for top.
Head: 18 rows.

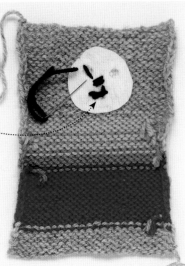

Sew from the front to position the features correctly.

Make the toy as for the knitten on pages 15–16.

For a rounded head effect, gather the top of the head.

Continue to sew the edges together.

Making ears

1

Cast on 8 stitches.

Work 6 rows in stockinette stitch.

2

Cut the yarn, thread it on to a needle, and collect up the stitches.

3

Pull the threaded needle all the way through the loops.

Pull the yarn tightly to gather the loops.

To stop the gather from loosening, sew the yarn back and forth to secure.

Thread the loose end on to a needle.

Use the loose end to sew the ear to the head.

**How tall
are the Teds?**

Li'l Ted stands 7in (18cm)
high and Big Ted is
13in (33cm) tall.

Li'l Ted

From simple knit stitch comes Little Ted, or Li'l Ted to his friends. He and Big Ted are made from five strips of basic knitting and lots of extra character!

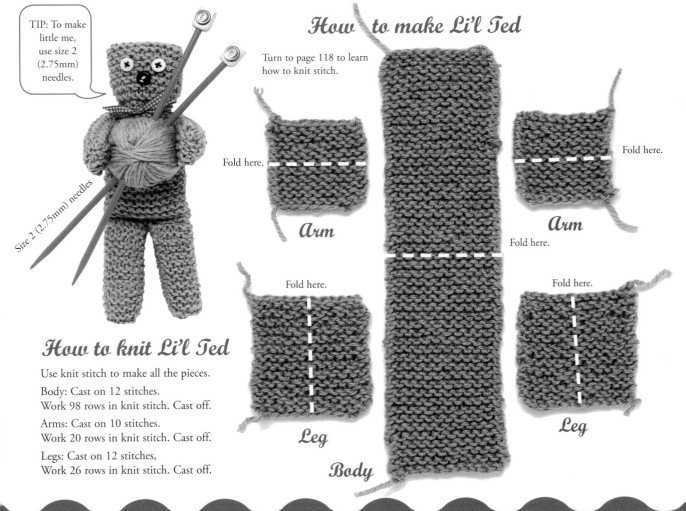

TIP: To make little me, use size 2 (2.75mm) needles.

Size 2 (2.75mm) needles

How to make Li'l Ted

Turn to page 118 to learn how to knit stitch.

Fold here.

Arm

Fold here.

Arm

Fold here.

Fold here.

Leg

Fold here.

Leg

Body

How to knit Li'l Ted

Use knit stitch to make all the pieces.

Body: Cast on 12 stitches.
Work 98 rows in knit stitch. Cast off.

Arms: Cast on 10 stitches.
Work 20 rows in knit stitch. Cast off.

Legs: Cast on 12 stitches,
Work 26 rows in knit stitch. Cast off.

Follow me, Li'l Ted! Bend and stretch.

Keep up, Li'l Ted. Run, step, and jump.

1

Fold the pieces in half, as shown on the previous page.

Sew neatly using whipstitch (page 114).

Using a tapestry needle, sew up the sides, leaving one end open.

2

Fill all the pieces—but not too full. Ted has to move his arms and legs.

Turn all the pieces inside out.

3

Attach the arms about a third of the way down the body.

Attach the legs from the corners of the body.

Sew neatly using whipstitch (page 114).

4

Using a sewing needle and thread, sew on his eyes and nose.

Tie a ribbon around the body above the arms to make a head and neck.

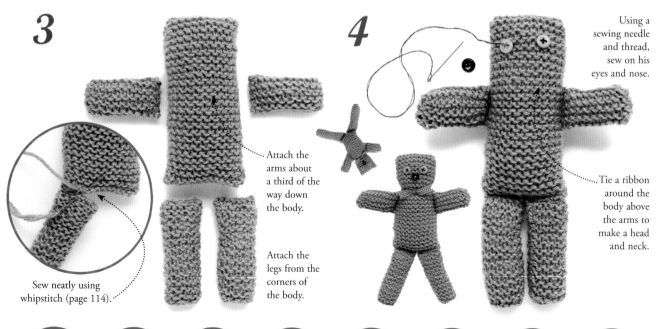

Steady, Li'l Ted! Don't go crazy...

Ta daaaaa!

For Big Ted you will need

- Size 6 (4mm) knitting needles
- Other materials as for Li'l Ted on page 22

How to knit Big Ted

Use knit stitch to make all the pieces.
Body: Cast on 20 stitches. Work 136 rows in knit stitch. Cast off.
Arms: Cast on 15 stitches. Work 32 rows in knit stitch. Cast off.
Legs: Cast on 20 stitches. Work 40 rows in knit stitch. Cast off.

Ted ideas

Use other colors of yarn to make Ted. He can be blue or green or even pink! Try making a multicolored Ted, either out of variegated yarn or from leftover scraps of yarn.

Odd bods

Pair up any mateless gloves to create these curious creatures. These three look like they're snug and warm, as if they're each wearing a sweater.

1 Turn the gloves inside out, and cut off the middle fingers and thumbs. Sew up the finger and thumb holes to close them.

Cut off the middle fingers and thumb.

2 Fill the ears or leave them floppy.

Fill all the pieces to make the head, body, arms, and tail.

3 Attach the head to the body: tuck one glove into the top of the other glove and pin in position.

Sew on the arms and tail.

4 Sew on buttons for eyes.

Stitch on the felt nose and embroider the mouth.

TOP TIP
If the head glove is too long, cut off some of the cuff for a better fit.

For the ears, leave them as they are or fold them over and secure them in place with a few stitches.

A box of monkeys

Kick off your old socks and bring a sock monkey to life. See those socks transform into a mischievous monkey—the smaller the socks, the cuter the monkey will be.

Here is the pattern for dividing two socks to create one sock monkey.

Arm x 2

Nose

Tail

Ear

Ear

Body and legs

=

Large or small socks?

Have fun using old or new socks to make your monkeys. Tiny socks make sweet babies, small socks can be children, and big socks are best for adults.

How to make a monkey

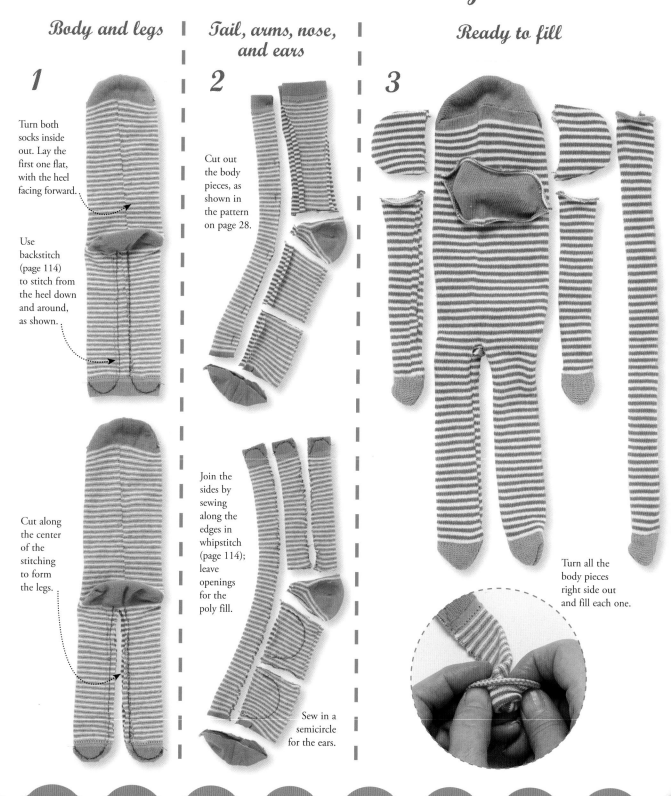

Body and legs

1

Turn both socks inside out. Lay the first one flat, with the heel facing forward.

Use backstitch (page 114) to stitch from the heel down and around, as shown.

Cut along the center of the stitching to form the legs.

Tail, arms, nose, and ears

2

Cut out the body pieces, as shown in the pattern on page 28.

Join the sides by sewing along the edges in whipstitch (page 114); leave openings for the poly fill.

Sew in a semicircle for the ears.

Ready to fill

3

Turn all the body pieces right side out and fill each one.

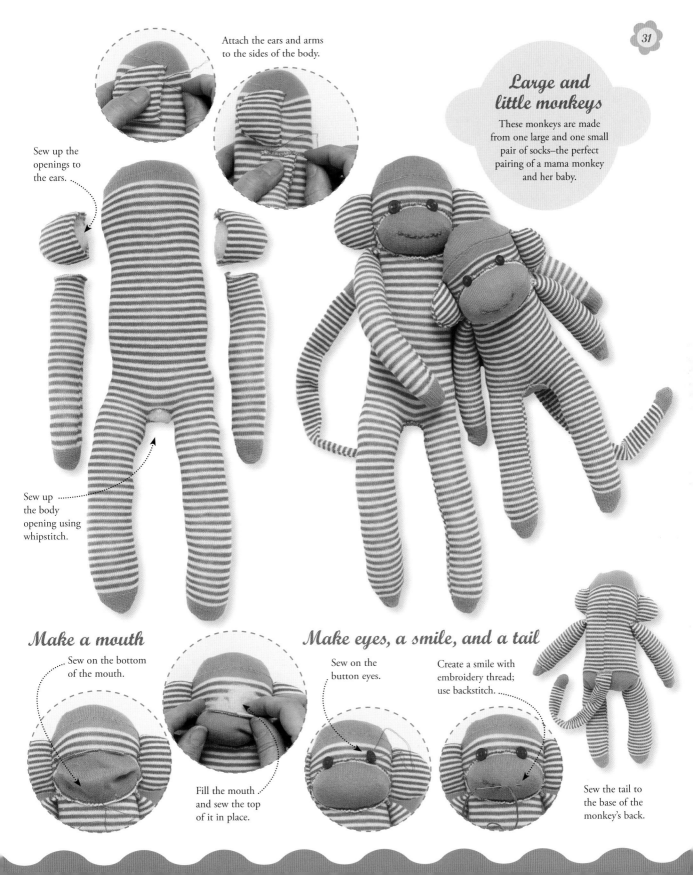

Attach the ears and arms to the sides of the body.

Large and little monkeys

These monkeys are made from one large and one small pair of socks—the perfect pairing of a mama monkey and her baby.

Sew up the openings to the ears.

Sew up the body opening using whipstitch.

Make a mouth

Sew on the bottom of the mouth.

Fill the mouth and sew the top of it in place.

Make eyes, a smile, and a tail

Sew on the button eyes.

Create a smile with embroidery thread; use backstitch.

Sew the tail to the base of the monkey's back.

Ducklings

These ducks lay eggs with a suprise inside. The ducks' simple knitted shapes hide the secrets in their plump curves. A knitted ribbed edge keeps each secret tucked away.

You will need

- Small balls of DK-weight yarn
- Size 6 (4mm) knitting needles
- Sewing kit (page 112)
- Poly fill
- Beads for eyes
- Felt for the beak

_## How to knit the duck's body

_## Shape the body

Cast on 22 stitches.
Rows 1–3 Knit 1, purl 1
(stockinette stitch) to the end of
each row.
Row 4 Knit 1, make 1, then knit
to the end (23 stitches).
Rows 5–18 Work as Row 4,
continuing to add a stitch to each
row (up to 36 stitches).

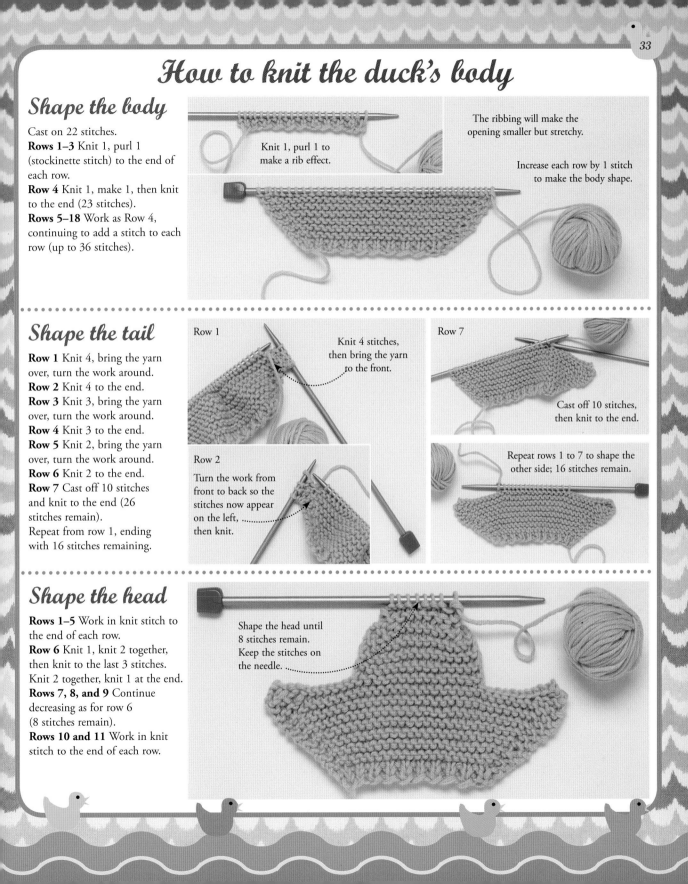

Knit 1, purl 1 to
make a rib effect.

The ribbing will make the
opening smaller but stretchy.

Increase each row by 1 stitch
to make the body shape.

Shape the tail

Row 1 Knit 4, bring the yarn
over, turn the work around.
Row 2 Knit 4 to the end.
Row 3 Knit 3, bring the yarn
over, turn the work around.
Row 4 Knit 3 to the end.
Row 5 Knit 2, bring the yarn
over, turn the work around.
Row 6 Knit 2 to the end.
Row 7 Cast off 10 stitches
and knit to the end (26
stitches remain).
Repeat from row 1, ending
with 16 stitches remaining.

Row 1

Knit 4 stitches,
then bring the yarn
to the front.

Row 2

Turn the work from
front to back so the
stitches now appear
on the left,
then knit.

Row 7

Cast off 10 stitches,
then knit to the end.

Repeat rows 1 to 7 to shape the
other side; 16 stitches remain.

Shape the head

Rows 1–5 Work in knit stitch to
the end of each row.
Row 6 Knit 1, knit 2 together,
then knit to the last 3 stitches.
Knit 2 together, knit 1 at the end.
Rows 7, 8, and 9 Continue
decreasing as for row 6
(8 stitches remain).
Rows 10 and 11 Work in knit
stitch to the end of each row.

Shape the head until
8 stitches remain.
Keep the stitches on
the needle.

33

How to make the duck's body

1 Cut the yarn, leaving a 6in (15cm) length. ..... Thread an embroidery needle and pick up the stitches from the knitting needle.

2 Collect up all the stitches and pull the thread all the way through the loops.

3 Pull the yarn tightly to gather up the knitting.

Sew in this loose end as well.

Sew along the edge to join the two sides together.

4 Fill the head area only.

Put in a small amount of filling.

5 Adjust the filling to make a head and neck shape.

Place the surprise gift inside the duck.

6 Beads for eyes

Cut out the felt beak.

Adjust the knitting to make a good duck shape with a perky tail.

7 Sew the beak in place.

Sew on the bead eyes and shape the beak.

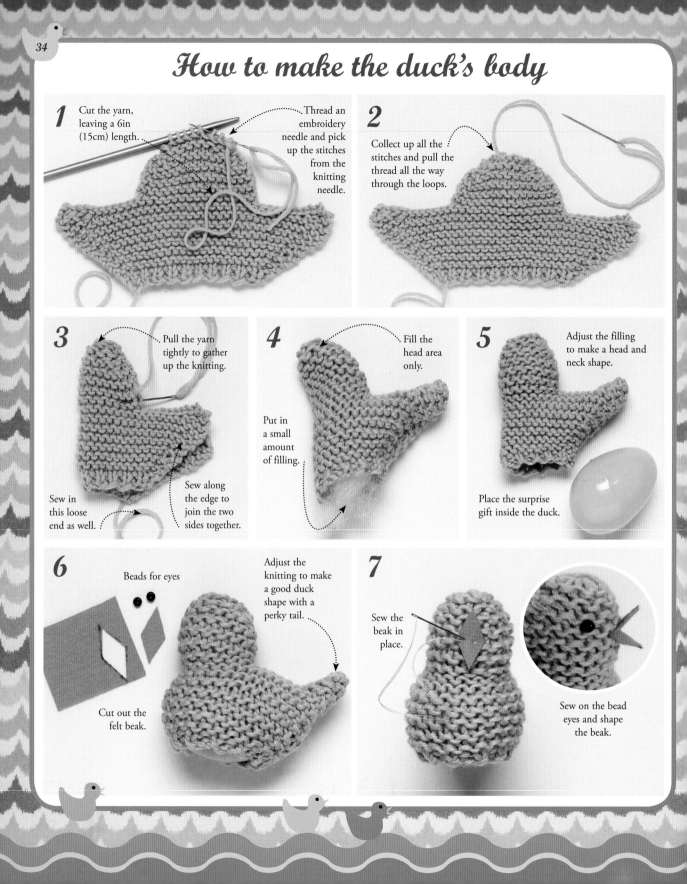

Full of surprises

These plastic egg-shaped containers are just right for small gifts, and they fit perfectly inside the ducks. Alternatively, wrap a small package and tuck it inside.

2

Friends in felt

Pocket pets

Rover

These little critters are all made from the same basic template design. Change the ears, beaks, and snouts to create all kinds of different pals.

Basic body shape for all the pets

Trace over the shapes to make a paper pattern. Turn to page 40 to see how.

Pinky Pig comes to visit

How to make Rover's house

Take a large juice carton and cut it down into a cube shape. Cut out a door. Cover the sides and roof with felt.

Stand the house on a grassy felt mat.

Cut a strip of green felt with a spiked edge to create flower stems.

Ribbit

Pinky

Sassy

Patch

Li'l Chick

Rover

Red

Kitty

You will need
• 4in x 3½in (10cm x 8cm) pieces of different-colored felt for bodies
• Felt scraps for noses and eyes
• Sewing kit (page 112)
• Poly fill

Tie a key ring to a length of ribbon and sew the ribbon to the head of the pet.

Working pets

Keep your pets as little creatures in your pockets or give them a job to do. Make them into key chains or use them to decorate bags. Alternatively, sew a pin to your pet's back and it becomes a brooch.

Sew a safety pin to the back to make a brooch.

How to make a paper pattern

Place tracing paper over the picture on the page. Trace over each of the features separately—the basic body shape, the ears, and any other features. Cut these out and pin them to the felt. Use this method to make your big pet, too.

First, trace the body shape, then the ears, patch, and collar.

Cut out each shape.

Use this method to make the body shape for the other pets.

How to make Rover

Use this method to make all the pets. It's easier to sew the face and nose to the front piece before attaching it to the back shape.

1

Pin the paper to the felt.

Cut 2 body shapes.

Cut one of each of the ears, patch, and collar.

2

Leave an opening at the top for the filling.

Attach the patch and sew to the face.

Take one piece of felt body shape.

3

Pin the front and back together.

Stitch the two body pieces together with whipstitch (page 114).

4

Add the filling.

Continue stitching to close the opening.

Work the stuffing into the paws.

5

Wrap the collar around the neck and sew in place.

Alternatively, use fabric glue to secure the collar.

6

Stitch the ears to the top of the head.

Make a large Rover

Create a mommy dog for your
little tyke.

Trace over the
template shown
here and follow
the instructions for
making the little pet.

Use this template to
make larger versions
of all your pets.

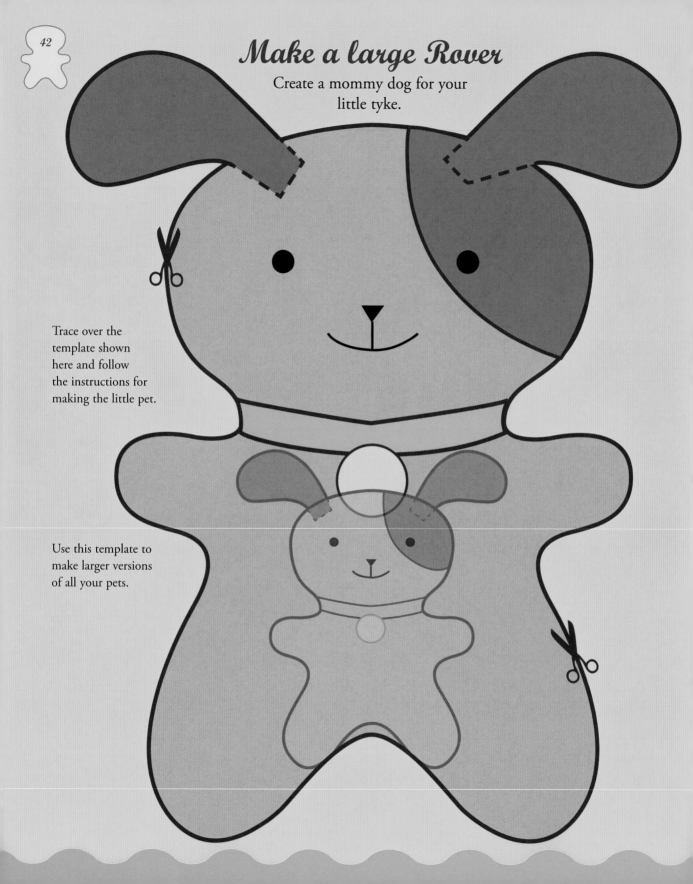

To make the ears stand up better, sew two pieces of felt together.

Little and large Rover

Large pets make great cuddly stuffed animals, and they don't require any more work to make than the little guys.

Place the sling straps around the large pet's neck and sew the ends of the straps together.

Cut lengths of felt 6in x ½in (15cm x 1cm) for the straps.

Make a sling

Cut a piece of felt 2½in x 4in (6cm x 10cm). Fold over the lower edge and sew up the side using whipstitch (page 114).

Make sure that your little pet fits comfortably in the sling. You may need to adjust the dimensions slightly.

Big pets

Match your pocket pets to their bigger friends.

How to make bags

Cut out a piece of felt larger than the size of the pet. Shape the felt and sew the sides together. Finally, sew on the felt straps. See the previous page for more about sizes.

Tip

To make the ears and eyes stand up straight, double the thickness of the felt and sew the edges together.

Cut a zigzag edge for a broken shell effect.

Add a felt stem and leaf.

Big Chick

with L'il Chick in an egg-shaped bag.

Big Pinky

with Pinky in an apple-shaped bag.

Each little pet has its own carry bag, just the right size.

How to make big pets

Follow the instructions on the previous pages. Enlarge the basic "large pet" template, draw paper templates for the ears, eyes, and other features. Sew the felt pieces together, as shown for the small pocket pet on page 41.

Cut the felt into a lily-pad leaf shape.

Backstitch the whiskers and eyelashes.

Add a felt lily to finish the bag.

Use running stitch for the veins of the leaf.

A plain bag, as used for the small Rover.

Big Ribbit

with Ribbit in a lily-pad-shaped bag.

Big Blue Cat

with Blue Cat in a sling-shaped carrier.

Mobile owls

Twirling and twisting, these mobiles work just as well on their own as they do in a group. Each owl is self-contained in its own hoop.

You will need

- Felt for body just smaller than the embroidery hoop, and scraps of colorful felt for wings, feet, and face
- Sewing kit (page 112) • Poly fill
- Buttons for eyes • 1¼ yards (1m) cotton fabric or ribbon
- 5½in (14cm) wooden embroidery hoop • Ribbon to hang

Owl template

Trace over the shapes to make a paper pattern. Turn to page 40 for instructions.

How to make an owl

Prepare all the felt pieces using the template on page 46.

1 Take one body piece of felt and attach the features using whipstitch (page 114).

2 Sew the wings and feet to the back of the felt.

Make the stitches neat and small.

3 Sew the front and back body pieces together.

Leave an opening at the bottom.

4 Fill the owl shape from the bottom and sew closed.

5 Take a strip of patterned fabric 1in (2.5cm) wide and wrap it around the hoop. Hold it in place with a few stitches.

Wooden embroidery hoop

6 Attach the owl by sewing a length of thread to the head and sew the other end to the fabric on the hoop.

The owl should swing freely in its hoop.

Tie a length of ribbon to the hoop and hang the mobile.

Cozy cats

These are two contented cats.
Their simple, quirky shape and flat base allow them to sit together very happily.

Little cat

Cat body

Trace over the shape to make a paper pattern.

Cat base

1 Pin the two felt shapes together.

Sew the shapes together with whipstitch (page 114), leaving the bottom open.

2 Fill the cat shape from the bottom.

Pin the base to the body and whipstitch in place.

3 Add buttons for eyes and pink felt for ears.

Sew on the features to finish your cat.

Fat cats

To make a bigger cat, simply enlarge the template on a photocopier or scanner. Use the copies as your paper pattern. This big cat was made by copying the template at 200 percent.

You will need

2 felt shapes for the body, each 5¼in x 4¾in (13cm x 12cm)

Sewing kit (page 112), buttons for eyes, felt ears, fabric motif, and sewing thread

1 felt shape for the base, 3½in x 2½in (10cm x 6cm)

Spring chickens

Make flocks of colorful birds. This busy clutch of chicks are made from bright scraps of felt. The wire legs give each one its own individual character.

You will need
- Colorful felt • 3ft (1m) plastic-covered wire • Poly fill
- Embroidery thread
- Sewing kit (page 112)

How to make a chick

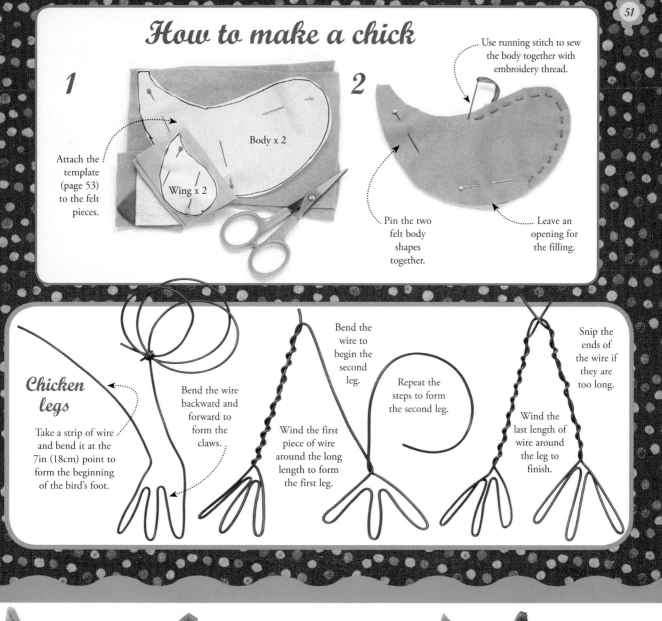

1

Attach the template (page 53) to the felt pieces.

Body x 2

Wing x 2

2

Use running stitch to sew the body together with embroidery thread.

Pin the two felt body shapes together.

Leave an opening for the filling.

Chicken legs

Take a strip of wire and bend it at the 7in (18cm) point to form the beginning of the bird's foot.

Bend the wire backward and forward to form the claws.

Wind the first piece of wire around the long length to form the first leg.

Bend the wire to begin the second leg.

Repeat the steps to form the second leg.

Wind the last length of wire around the leg to finish.

Snip the ends of the wire if they are too long.

Cheep, cheep

3

Fill the bird until it feels soft but still a little firm.

After positioning the legs (see below), add more poly fill to puff out the stomach.

4

Use running stitch (page 114) to sew on the wing with embroidery thread.

Continue to sew the features on each side.

Push the legs into the filling as far as they will go. Hold the legs firmly between your thumb and fingers.

Sew up the opening, stitching tightly aroung the legs.

Bend the feet at the ankle.

Adjust the angle of the feet so the chick can stand.

Chirp, chirp

Create a chirping chicken

The chick's simple body shape is mirrored in the shape of its wings, and is finished off with a beady eye and a triangular beak. For a bright birdie, use contrasting colors of felt.

Mice made easy

Cut a disk from pretty cotton fabric. Fold it in half, and you have a charming little mouse shape.

Any lightweight cotton or felt fabric will work.

Cut a disk of fabric 4½in (11cm) wide.

You will need
• 5¼in x 5¼in (13cm x 13cm) square of cotton fabric for body
• Felt for ears • Beads for eyes
• Sewing kit (page 112)
• String for tail • Poly fill

1
Make ear shapes from felt.
Pin the fabric together.
Fold the fabric in half.

2
Sew in the ears as you go.
Sew along the edge, nearly to the end.
With embroidery thread, sew in running stitch (page 114) from the nose end.
Fill the mouse's body.

3
Tie a knot in the end of the string.
Place the tail in the opening and stitch it in place.

4
Use sewing thread to sew on beads for the eyes.
Finish sewing and fasten off.

Mix and match mice

Play with the colors of fabric, felt, and thread that you use. If you don't want to match colors, mix them to create stunning and wacky clashes.

Sewing tip

When sewing on the beads for the eyes, begin by sewing one eye in place before taking the needle through the fabric to the other side of the head and attaching the other eye. This technique makes the eyes press into the fabric.

Gift ideas

• **Brooch:** Sew a safety pin to the back of a mouse.
• **Pin cushion:** Add straight pins and include your mouse in a sewing kit.
• **Sweet-smelling mice:** Mix dried lavender into the filling to create a fragrant gift.

Minimals

What do you call a mini animal?

A minimal! These plumped-up little pillows
are not much bigger than your thumb.

You will need

- Colorful scraps of felt
- Poly fill • Embroidery thread
- Sewing kit (page 112)

Pin the
template
(page 58)
to the
felt.

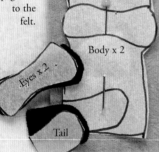

Eyes x 2

Body x 2

Tail

Decorate
the front
first.

Use embroidery
thread to add
features.

Sew the
front and
back together
with sewing
thread.

Fill the tiny
body with a
small amount
of filling.

Finish by
sewing up
the base.

Little boxes
of minimals

Empty matchboxes make
cozy homes for your
miniature animals. Decorate
the boxes with colorful
fabrics that match your
little friends.

Boxes of minimals

We also make beautiful brooches.

Use these templates to create your own matchbox-sized minimals. See pages 56–57.

Minimal mobiles

For a more natural effect, use twigs from the yard to hang your minimals and maximals. Sew a length of yarn to the top of each one and tie it to a twig.

Wild ones

Maximize your minimals
to create a wild bunch of creatures.
Increase the template to 150 percent
and make the big critters in the same
way as you would the little ones.

Bees and bugs

Sew swarms of bees and bugs! Get creative with felt and blanket stitch and make the cutest bees and bugs on Earth!

You will need

- 5in x 6½in (11½cm x 16cm) piece red felt
- 4in x 5in (10cm x 11½cm) piece black felt
- Scraps of white felt
- Sewing kit (page 112)
- Poly fill

Pin the template to the felt and cut out the shapes.

Use for body and base.

Cut out the spots and eyes.

Trace over the bug template. Cut one base in black, two body shapes in red, six black spots, and two black and white eyes.

1

First, sew the features to the ladybug body.

2

Sew the base and one half of the body together. Use blanket stitch (page 115).

Black base for bug

3

Sew the other half of the body to the base in the same way.

4

Sew the two body shapes partway together.

Add the filling.

5

Once filled, sew up the opening.

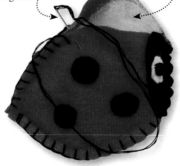

How to make bees

Cut out the body shapes, face, and eyes in the same way as for the spotted bugs. Make stripes from black felt and two white felt wings. Sew on the stripes before stitching the pieces together. Add wings at the end.

3

Sew cute

Dog's best friends

Sew some pretty pups. Use the fold of the fabric in the back to give your little doggies a nice curvy shape. Make ones that are small enough to fit in your hand or big enough to be comfy pillows.

DOGS IN TRANSIT
handle with care

You will need

- 6in x 9½in (14cm x 23cm) cotton fabric
- Felt scraps for ears and noses • Poly fill
- Buttons for eyes • Colorful thread for mouth • Sewing kit (page 112)

How to make friends

1

Fold fabric.

Place the edge of the paper against the fold.

Fold the fabric in half.

Pin the paper to the fabric and carefully cut around the dog shape.

2

Sew around the shape using backstitch (page 114).

Leave an opening for the filling.

3

Turn the dog shape right side out.

Fill the shape and carefully sew the opening closed.

Slip stitch (page 114).

Add the features

Eyes

Nose

Ears

Collar

Tail

Sew the ear to the top of the head.

Stitch on a mouth using backstitch (page 114).

To attach the nose, stitch backward and forward through the nose fabric and felt.

Wrap the felt collar around the neck and sew it in place with the button.

Attach the tail in the same way as the nose.

Find the pattern for Dog's best friends on page 68.

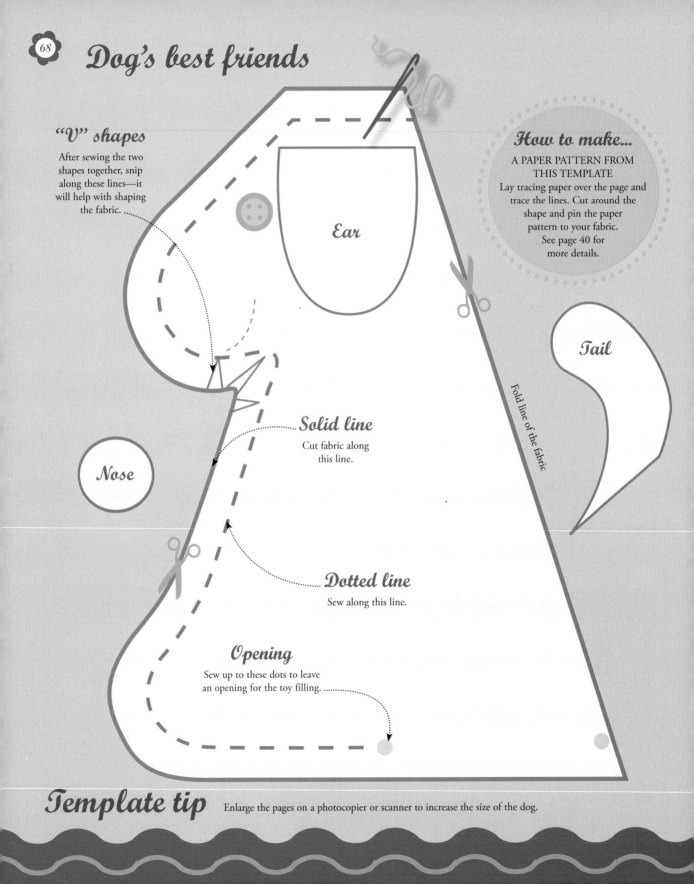

Dog's best friends

"V" shapes

After sewing the two shapes together, snip along these lines—it will help with shaping the fabric.

Ear

How to make...

A PAPER PATTERN FROM THIS TEMPLATE
Lay tracing paper over the page and trace the lines. Cut around the shape and pin the paper pattern to your fabric. See page 40 for more details.

Tail

Fold line of the fabric

Solid line

Cut fabric along this line.

Nose

Dotted line

Sew along this line.

Opening

Sew up to these dots to leave an opening for the toy filling.

Template tip
Enlarge the pages on a photocopier or scanner to increase the size of the dog.

Big dog pillow

Making bigger dogs is easy: copy or scan the templete page and increase the template size to 200 percent. Use the paper printout for your pattern. Follow the instructions for making the small dog.

This dog is made at 200 percent.

Pretty birdies

Gather up pieces of patterned fabric to create these cute little birds. Use embroidery stitches to give the birds features and have fun with the fabric print, following the flower shapes to create a really special effect.

How to make a bird

Patterned
cotton fabric

Buttons
and ribbons

Embroidery
thread

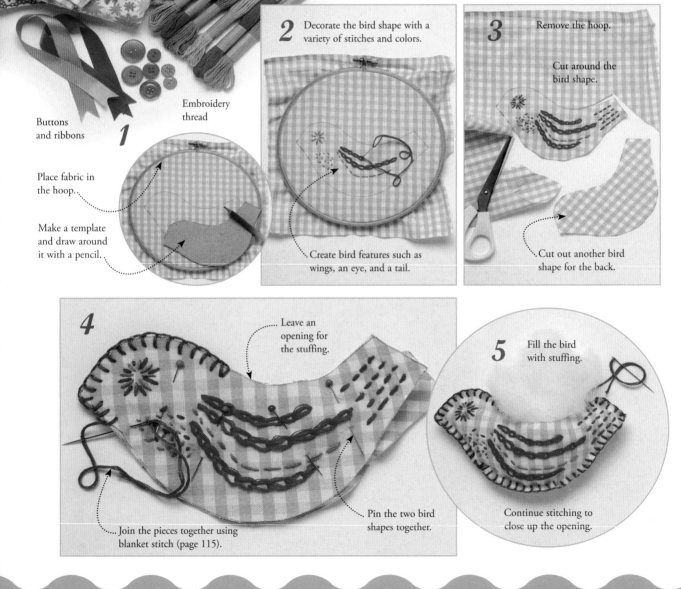

1

Place fabric in
the hoop.

Make a template
and draw around
it with a pencil.

2 Decorate the bird shape with a
variety of stitches and colors.

Create bird features such as
wings, an eye, and a tail.

3 Remove the hoop.

Cut around the
bird shape.

Cut out another bird
shape for the back.

4

Leave an
opening for
the stuffing.

Join the pieces together using
blanket stitch (page 115).

Pin the two bird
shapes together.

5 Fill the bird
with stuffing.

Continue stitching to
close up the opening.

Sewing tip

Use the design on the patterned fabric to guide your stitches. Follow the outline of the petals and add chain-stitch leaves using threads in contrasting colors. Finish with buttons for eyes.

Flying birds

To make hanging birds, cut a length of ribbon 8in (20cm) long, fold it in half, and sew it to the bird. Add a button for a decorative touch.

Bunny girls

Rag-doll rabbits offer a crafty twist on the classic rag doll.
Dress these little ladies up and design a fashion collection just for them.

You will need

- 12in x 24in (30cm x 60cm) piece cotton fabric for doll • Sewing kit (page 112) • Poly fill • 16in x 10in (40cm x 25cm) piece patterned cotton fabric for dress • Felt for eyes • Rickrack and ribbon

The bunnies get together for a cup of tea

Dressed up and ready to go

- **Dresses:** Make the bunnies pretty dresses with matching headscarves. Decorate the dresses with strips of rickrack and ribbon.
- **Bags:** Add matching handbags to your bunny's wardrobe. For each bag, sew two pieces of felt together and finish with a ribbon strap.

74

To ensure a nice shape when the bunny is turned right side out, snip the fabric at the notches.

Right leg x 2

The dotted lines show where to sew.

Left leg x 2

Bunny's body

Lay tracing paper over the page and carefully draw over all the lines, including the dotted lines. Cut out the paper shapes and use them as your pattern. For more about making paper patterns, turn to page 40.

Body x 2

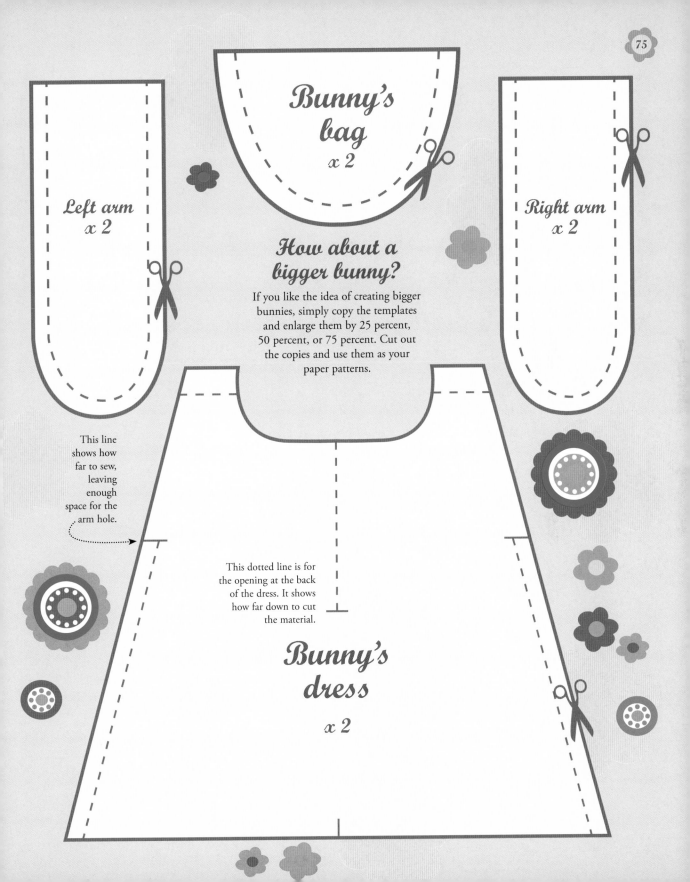

Left arm
x 2

Bunny's bag
x 2

How about a bigger bunny?

If you like the idea of creating bigger bunnies, simply copy the templates and enlarge them by 25 percent, 50 percent, or 75 percent. Cut out the copies and use them as your paper patterns.

Right arm
x 2

This line shows how far to sew, leaving enough space for the arm hole.

This dotted line is for the opening at the back of the dress. It shows how far down to cut the material.

Bunny's dress
x 2

How to make a bunny

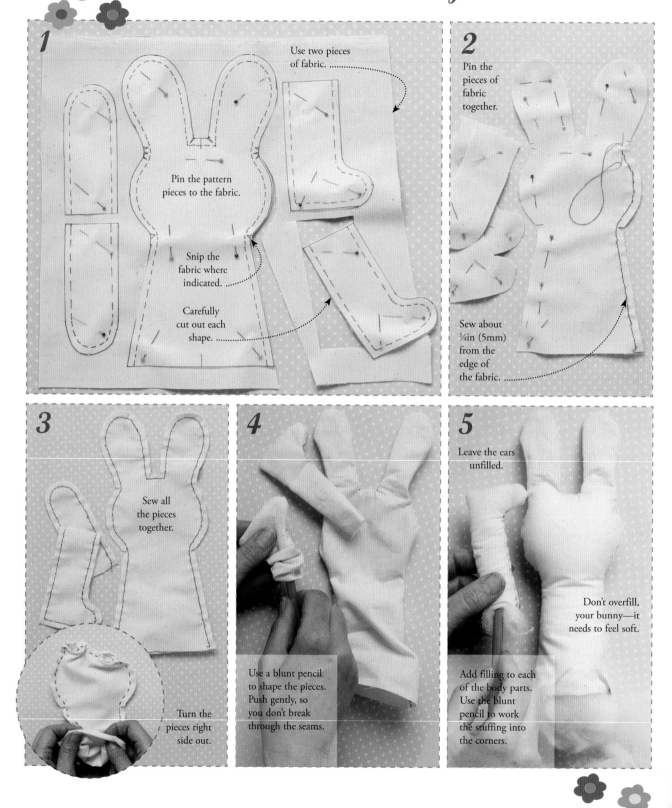

1

Pin the pattern pieces to the fabric.

Use two pieces of fabric.

Snip the fabric where indicated.

Carefully cut out each shape.

2

Pin the pieces of fabric together.

Sew about ¼in (5mm) from the edge of the fabric.

3

Sew all the pieces together.

Turn the pieces right side out.

4

Use a blunt pencil to shape the pieces. Push gently, so you don't break through the seams.

5

Leave the ears unfilled.

Don't overfill, your bunny—it needs to feel soft.

Add filling to each of the body parts. Use the blunt pencil to work the stuffing into the corners.

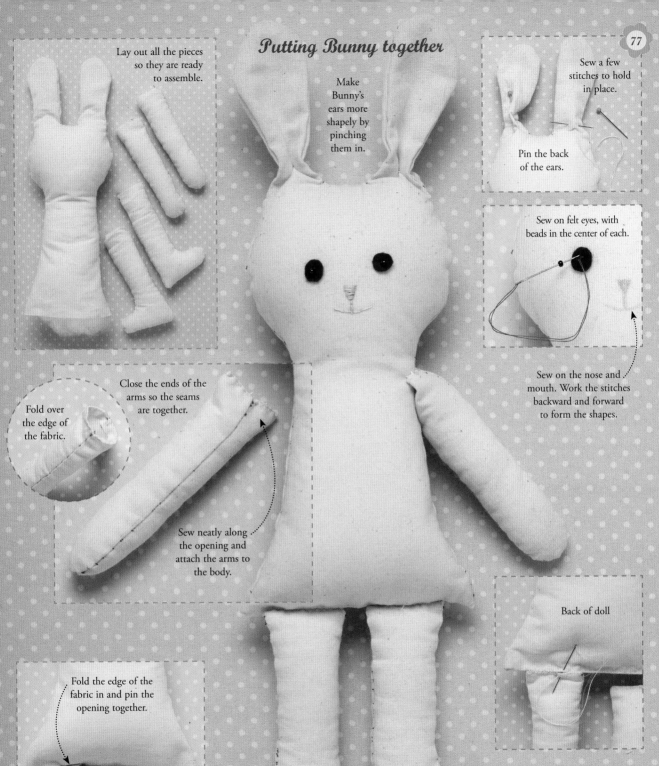

Putting Bunny together

Lay out all the pieces so they are ready to assemble.

Make Bunny's ears more shapely by pinching them in.

Sew a few stitches to hold in place.

Pin the back of the ears.

Sew on felt eyes, with beads in the center of each.

Sew on the nose and mouth. Work the stitches backward and forward to form the shapes.

Fold over the edge of the fabric.

Close the ends of the arms so the seams are together.

Sew neatly along the opening and attach the arms to the body.

Back of doll

Fold the edge of the fabric in and pin the opening together.

Sew the two edges together neatly.

Turn the doll over. Carefully sew the legs to the body using whipstitch (page 114).

For the dress and bag

You will need

- 2 x 6in x 6in (15cm x 15cm) pieces colorful cotton fabric
- Matching fabric for headscarf
- Sewing kit (page 112) • 2 x 2½in x 2½in (6cm x 6cm) pieces felt
- Felt scraps for eyes and motifs
- Ribbons

Handy tip

Use pinking shears (page 113) to cut out the dress. This gives the fabric pretty edges that don't need to be finished.

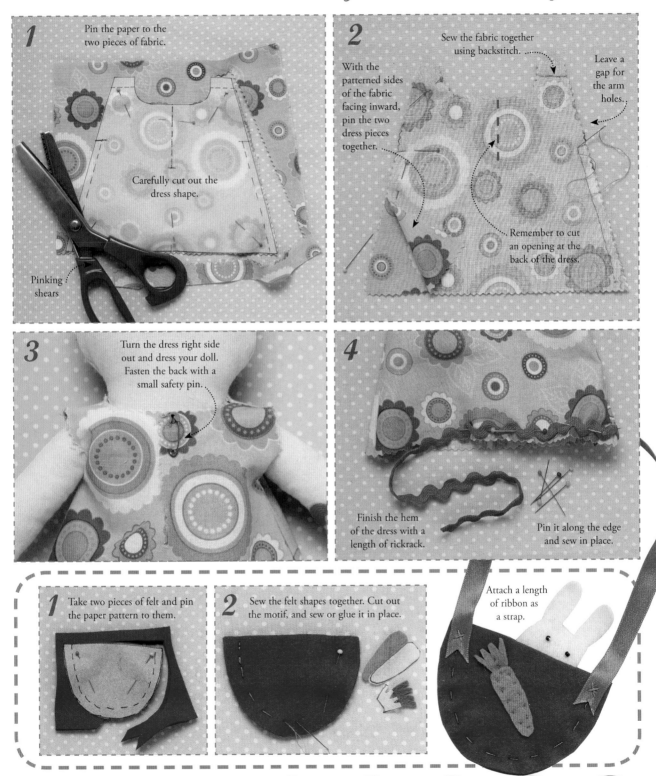

1 Pin the paper to the two pieces of fabric.

Carefully cut out the dress shape.

Pinking shears

2 With the patterned sides of the fabric facing inward, pin the two dress pieces together.

Sew the fabric together using backstitch.

Leave a gap for the arm holes.

Remember to cut an opening at the back of the dress.

3 Turn the dress right side out and dress your doll. Fasten the back with a small safety pin.

4 Finish the hem of the dress with a length of rickrack.

Pin it along the edge and sew in place.

1 Take two pieces of felt and pin the paper pattern to them.

2 Sew the felt shapes together. Cut out the motif, and sew or glue it in place.

Attach a length of ribbon as a strap.

Doodlephants

Who can resist doodling?

This project combines a stuffed animal and a doodled design, which is inspired by the medallions and flowers used on Indian fabrics. First, make a solid-colored elephant, then doodle away.

Draw your design directly on the fabric.

Use felt for the ears and tail.

Permanent markers

Pens to use

You don't need special fabric pens for this project. Permanent markers will work just as well.

Cut the end of the tail into thin strips.

Muslin or pale-colored cotton fabrics show off your doodles really well.

You will need
- 24in x 10in (60cm x 25cm) muslin or cotton fabric for body
- Gray felt for tail and ears
- Sewing kit (page 112)
- Permanent markers
- Poly fill
- Buttons for eyes

How to make an elephant

Follow the steps on page 82.

1

Fill the area with your design, leaving spaces that can be colored in.

2

Next, color in your design.

3 *Finished coloring?*

The great thing about doodling is that the design options are almost endless. There's nearly always a little space left that you can fill with a dot or a swirl.

Complete both sides of your elephant.

Find the pattern for doodlephants on page 84.

Make a plain elephant

1

Pin the template to two pieces of fabric and cut out both shapes.

2 Pin the two pieces together.

Use backstitch (page 114) to join the pieces. Leave an opening for the filling.

Sew about ¼in (5mm) from the edge.

3 Turn the elephant inside out.

Fill the elephant until it is soft, but still a little firm. Sew up the opening.

4

Ears

Tail

For the tail, fold a 4in x 1in (10cm x 2cm) piece of felt in half and stitch it together.

Cut an 8in x 3in (20cm x 8cm) piece of felt for the ears.

5 Lay the felt ears over the top of the elephant.

Stitch in place along the center.

6

Sew the tail in place at the back, across the seam.

Cut the end of the tail to create a fringe effect.

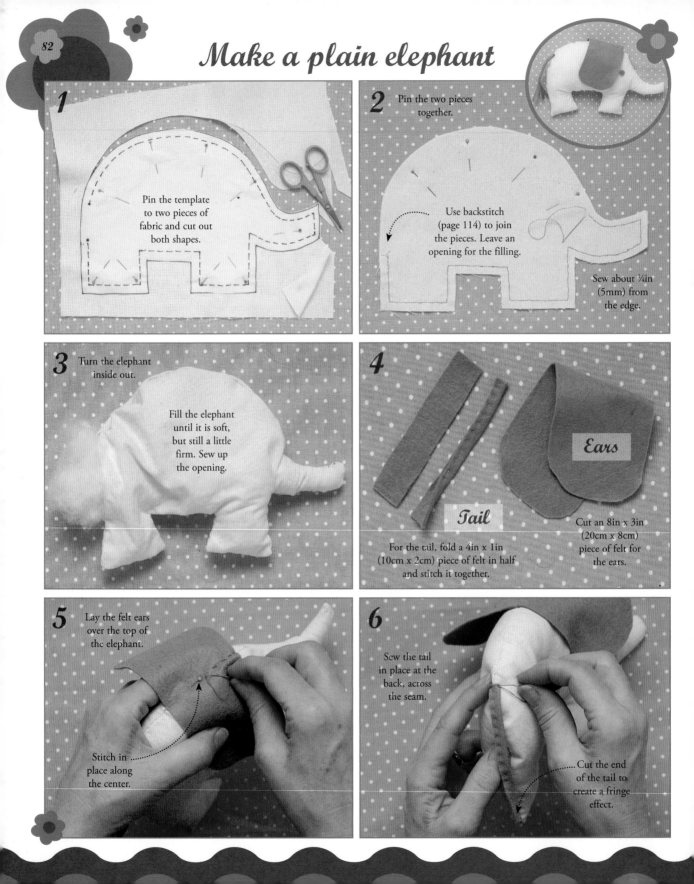

Cotton fabric

These elephants are made from muslin. Muslin is an inexpensive and versatile fabric. If you can't find it, any lightweight solid-colored cotton fabric will work just as well.

Opening

Sew up to these dots, leaving
an opening for the poly fill.

Fold

Doodlephant tail

Doodlephant

How to make...

A PAPER PATTERN FROM
THIS TEMPLATE
Lay tracing paper over the page and trace
over the outline. Cut around the shape
and pin the paper pattern to your fabric.
See page 40 for more details.

After sewing the two
shapes together, snip along
these lines—it will help
with shaping the fabric.

Dotted line

Sew along this line.

Solid line

Cut fabric out along
this line.

Doodlephant ears

Double thickness fabric.

Fold line of the fabric.

Fabric elephants Not just for doodling—these elephants look good in colorful cotton fabric, too.

Jumbo-sized elephants

Scan the template page from the book, increasing the size to 200 percent. Print the template and cut it out. Pin the paper pattern to the fabric and follow the instructions for making a doodlephant.

This elephant is made at **200** *percent*

Your little pony

With their swishing tails and soft manes, these ponies will take you back to your childhood. You'll have endless fun creating a stable full of little ponies.

You will need

- 2 x 8in x 8in (20cm x 20cm) pieces of cotton fabric
- Yarn • Tapestry needle
- Poly fill
- Felt and buttons for eyes and ears
- Sewing kit (page 112)

To make the tail

To make the long tail, cut 10 lengths of yarn 10in (24cm) long. Knot them together in the middle with a slip knot (page 116).

The mane is made from lengths of yarn 6in (15cm) long and sewn through the fabric to form a small tassel.

Use backstitch to create the mouth (page 114).

Finish off the eye with a button stitched over the eyelash.

Find the pattern
for your little pony on page 88.

Once the tail is in place, cut all the yarn to the same length.

How to make your pony

1 Pin the pattern to two pieces of fabric and carefully cut out the shape.

2 Turn the fabric so the pattern sides face each other.

Leave an opening at the top for the filling.

Using backstitch, sew around the shape ¼in (5mm) from the edge.

Turn the shape right side out and fill. Work the filling into all the corners and use slip stitch (page 114) to close the opening.

How to attach the mane

Insert the needle from the left and pull the yarn almost all the way through. Insert the needle from the right and pull the yarn through, leaving a loop.

Take the needle off the thread and adjust it so the ends are equal.

Sew the tail to the pony.

Sew the ears on both sides of the head. Apply the eyes in the same way.

Thread the ends of the yarn through the loop and pull.

Your little pony

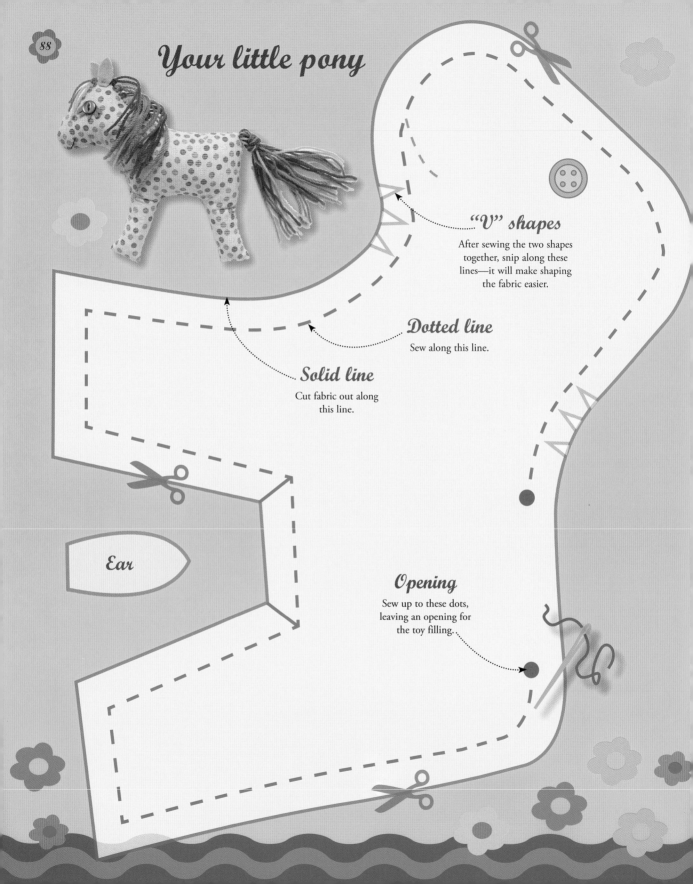

"V" shapes

After sewing the two shapes together, snip along these lines—it will make shaping the fabric easier.

Dotted line

Sew along this line.

Solid line

Cut fabric out along this line.

Ear

Opening

Sew up to these dots, leaving an opening for the toy filling.

Your pony friends

Use your pony template to make a whole herd of ponies. Experiment with cotton fabrics in different patterns.

Jolly Giraffe

Meet Jolly and Jill Giraffe.
Their simple design, which requires no complicated shaping, makes it easy for them to stand by themselves.

Lovely legs

Choose a fun fabric similar to Jolly's, since it resembles a real giraffe's coloring. For an extra-special effect, use a contrasting fabric for the inside of your giraffe's legs.

You will need

- 2 x 12in x 12in (30cm x 30cm) pieces cotton fabric for the body
- 8in x 9½in (20cm x 24cm) contrasting color fabric for inside legs
- Buttons for eyes and legs
- Felt for tail and ears
- Poly fill
- Sewing kit (page 112)

Find the pattern

for Jolly Giraffe on page 94

How to make a giraffe

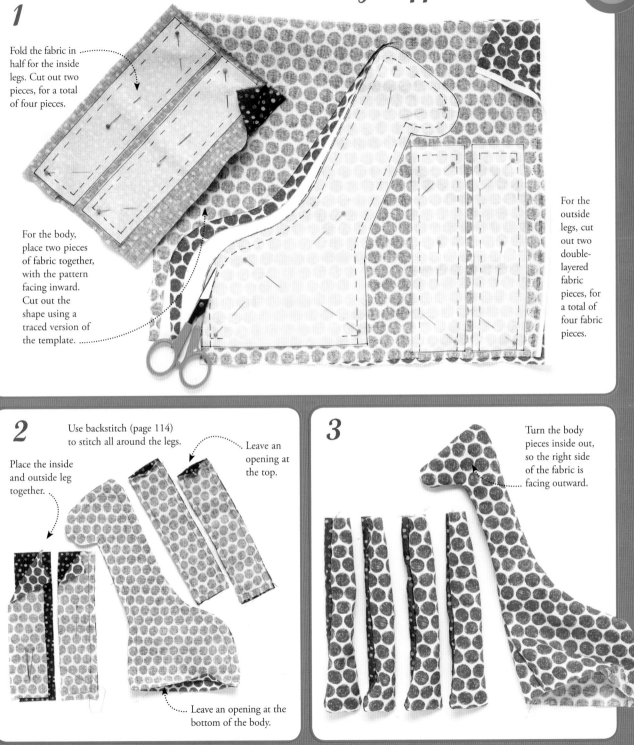

1

Fold the fabric in half for the inside legs. Cut out two pieces, for a total of four pieces.

For the body, place two pieces of fabric together, with the pattern facing inward. Cut out the shape using a traced version of the template.

For the outside legs, cut out two double-layered fabric pieces, for a total of four fabric pieces.

2

Use backstitch (page 114) to stitch all around the legs.

Leave an opening at the top.

Place the inside and outside leg together.

Leave an opening at the bottom of the body.

3

Turn the body pieces inside out, so the right side of the fabric is facing outward.

4

Fill all the body parts until they are soft, but firm.

Work the stuffing evenly into the head and neck.

5

To finish the legs, fold the top of the fabric over neatly and pin the openings together.

Sew the openings closed using slip stitch (page 114).

6

Fold in the edges of the fabric and sew up the opening using slip stitch.

Giraffes on the move

Because the legs are sewn on to the body separately, they can move independently. This allows you to position your giraffe into all kinds of poses.

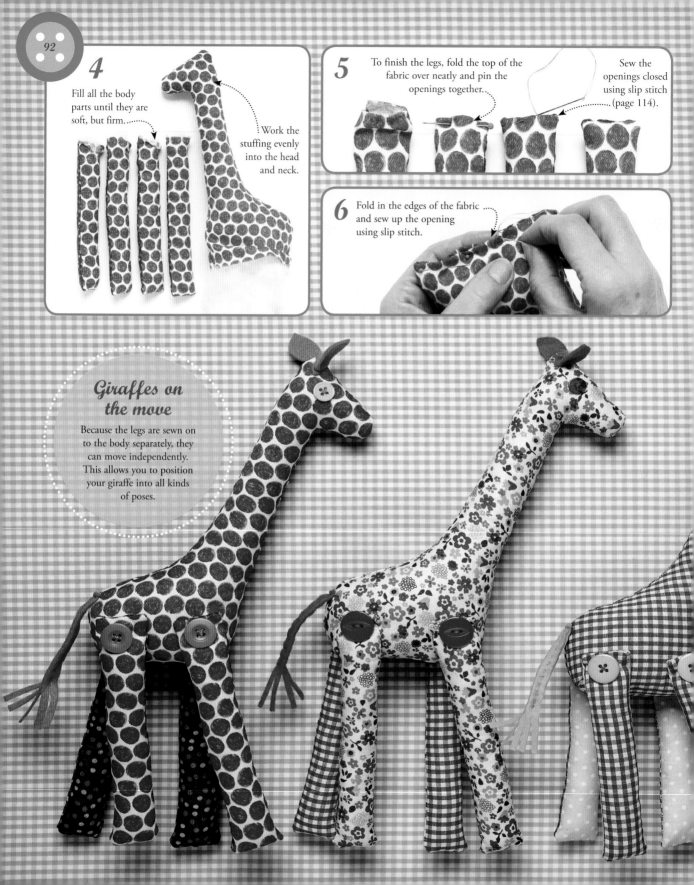

Assemble the giraffe

Shaping the body

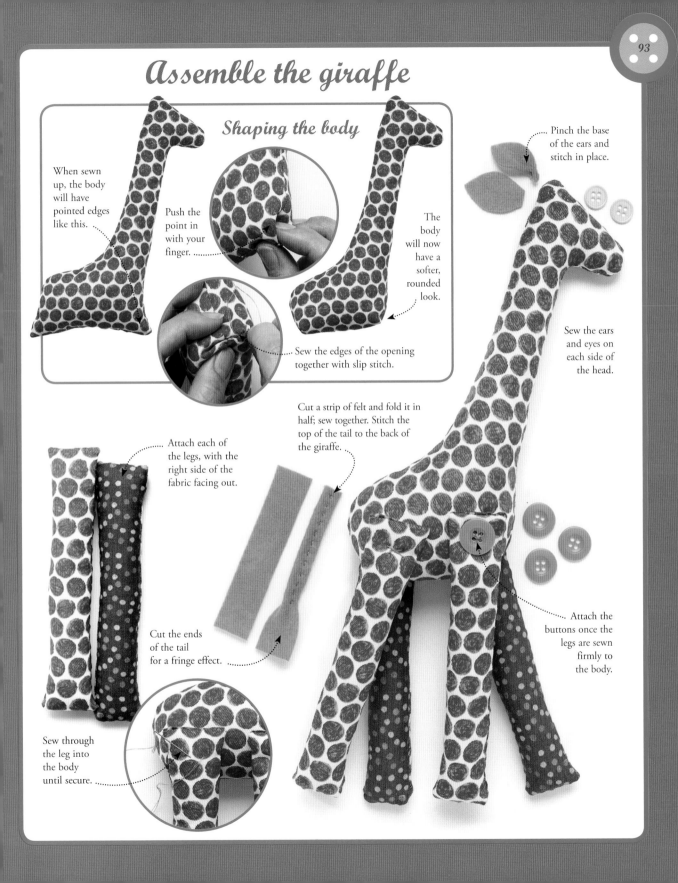

When sewn up, the body will have pointed edges like this.

Push the point in with your finger.

Sew the edges of the opening together with slip stitch.

The body will now have a softer, rounded look.

Pinch the base of the ears and stitch in place.

Sew the ears and eyes on each side of the head.

Attach each of the legs, with the right side of the fabric facing out.

Cut a strip of felt and fold it in half; sew together. Stitch the top of the tail to the back of the giraffe.

Cut the ends of the tail for a fringe effect.

Attach the buttons once the legs are sewn firmly to the body.

Sew through the leg into the body until secure.

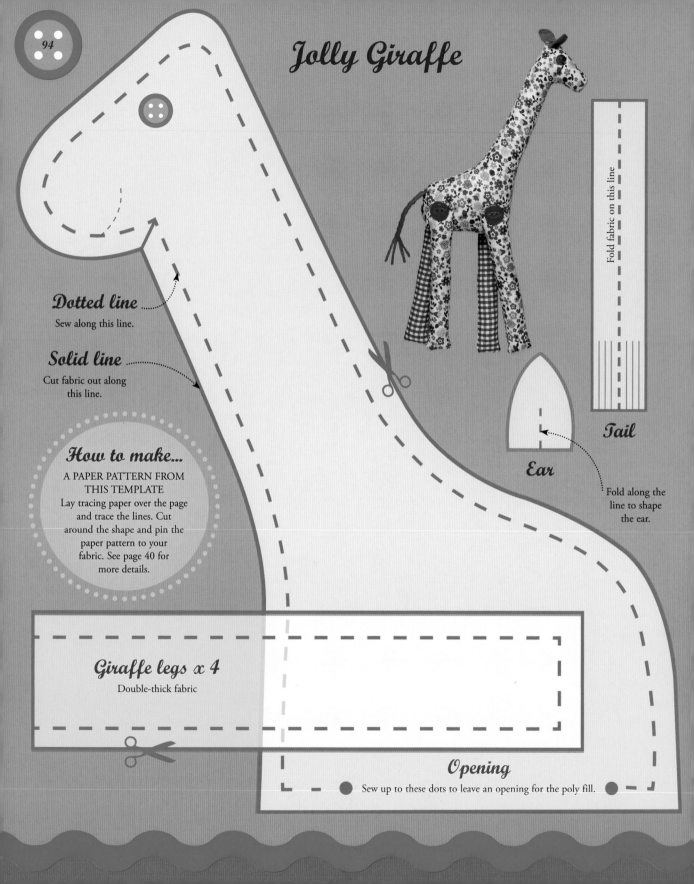

Jolly Giraffe

Dotted line
Sew along this line.

Solid line
Cut fabric out along this line.

How to make...
A PAPER PATTERN FROM THIS TEMPLATE
Lay tracing paper over the page and trace the lines. Cut around the shape and pin the paper pattern to your fabric. See page 40 for more details.

Fold fabric on this line

Tail

Ear

Fold along the line to shape the ear.

Giraffe legs x 4
Double-thick fabric

Opening
● Sew up to these dots to leave an opening for the poly fill. ●

You can make little guys, too.

Standing tall

Giraffes are usually tall... and taller. To make big giraffes, copy or scan the template page, increase the size to 150 percent, print it out, and make the big giraffes just as you would the little ones.

Cat's bed

Create a comfy cover for a sleepy toy.
Made from two different fabrics, this little patchwork
quilt is a super-easy design to put together.

You will need
- 2 pieces of contrasting fabric
- Paper • Felt for backing
- Sewing kit (page 112)
- Ribbon for decoration

How to assemble the patches

Cut out 9 paper squares
2in x 2in (5cm x 5cm)

Cut out 9 fabric squares
3in x 3in (7cm x 7cm)
Cut 5 squares of one fabric
and 4 of the other.

1 Place the paper in the
center of the fabric.

Fold the fabric over the
edge of the paper.

2 Sew the fabric to the paper
using large stitches.

3 Sew all the way
around.

Sew the squares
together.

Make the
stitches small
and neat.

Undo the basting
stitch and remove
the paper.

Cut the felt to
the same size as
the sewn patches.

Make the most of
the fabric designs by
putting them in the
center of the patch.

Carefully sew the
felt to the patches
using running stitch
(page 114).

Zzzzz...

Zzzz...

Handy tip

Adjust the size of your quilt in one of two ways: make more small square patches or enlarge the size of each square. Create a quilt as large as you like—just right for the size of your cat.

4

Animals
in stitches

Pictures in stitches

Big or small—make the same picture in different sizes by using fabrics of varying thread counts.

You will need

- 8-count and 14-count cross-stitch fabric
- Sewing kit (page 112)

Make a picture

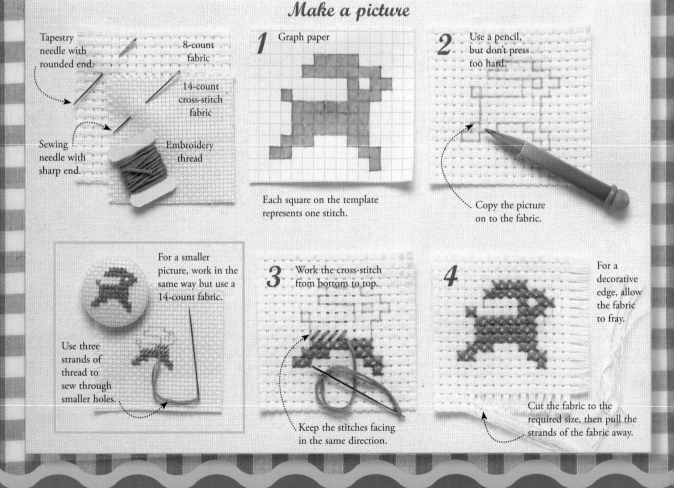

Tapestry needle with rounded end.

8-count fabric

14-count cross-stitch fabric

Sewing needle with sharp end.

Embroidery thread

1 Graph paper

Each square on the template represents one stitch.

2 Use a pencil, but don't press too hard.

Copy the picture on to the fabric.

For a smaller picture, work in the same way but use a 14-count fabric.

Use three strands of thread to sew through smaller holes.

3 Work the cross-stitch from bottom to top.

Keep the stitches facing in the same direction.

4 For a decorative edge, allow the fabric to fray.

Cut the fabric to the required size, then pull the strands of the fabric away.

See page 102
for templates.

Glue your pictures
to the front of
greeting cards.

Design your
own key
chain.

There are lots of ways you can use
your pictures. Add them to greeting
cards, or make buttons, box lids, or
key chains—all are perfect gifts.

Customize your
belongings by
attaching different-
sized pictures to them.
Create a matching set
in no time!

Animal patterns

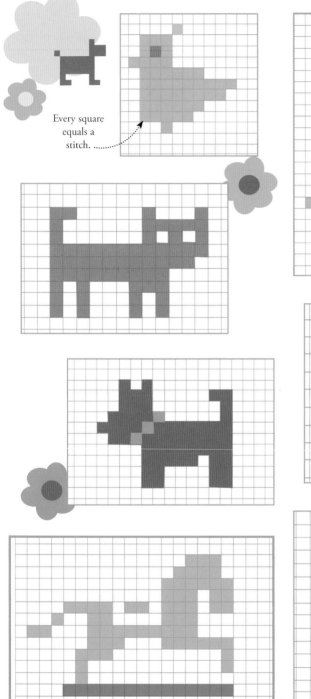

Every square equals a stitch.

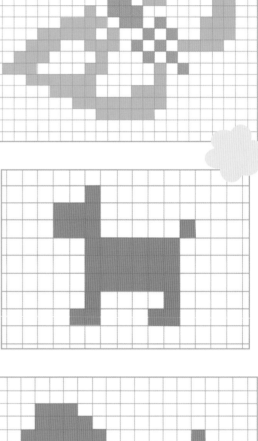

Fill in the gaps between the animals with cross-stitch patterns.

These hoops make perfect picture frames for your work. Fold the fabric behind the frame when you've finished sewing.

The big picture

Before enlarging a picture, first plan it out on graph paper. Then take a piece of 8-count fabric larger than the area of your design. Count out the squares on the fabric and begin stitching. When complete, cut around your work. Fray the edge to make an attractive border.

Follow the pattern

Center the design on the canvas and use the colored squares to position the stitches and match the colors. Begin stitching the main part of the image first, then work the other colors one at a time.

You will need

A piece of canvas
4in x 5in (10cm x 13cm)

Selection of tapestry yarn and needle

Felt pens

Pet portraits

Draw a picture of your favorite pet. With some pens and graph paper, turn the portrait into colored squares. No pets? No problem. Stitch this little cat instead. Just choose different-colored yarn if you want to change the color of the cat and background.

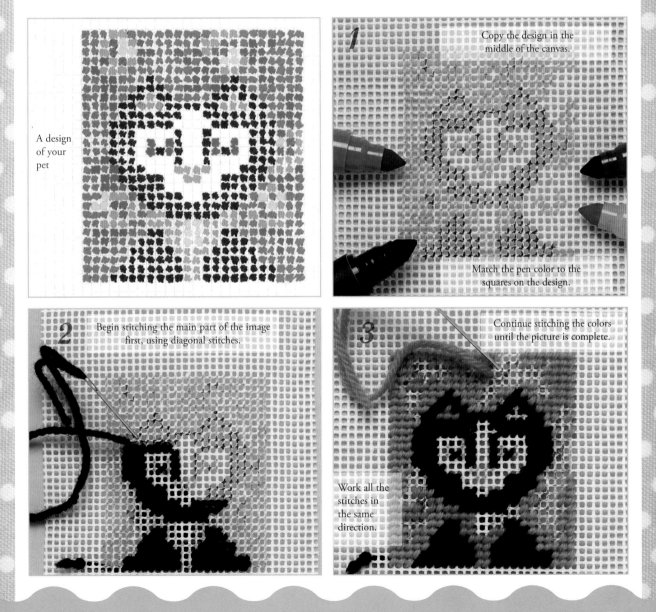

A design of your pet

1 Copy the design in the middle of the canvas.

Match the pen color to the squares on the design.

2 Begin stitching the main part of the image first, using diagonal stitches.

3 Continue stitching the colors until the picture is complete.

Work all the stitches in the same direction.

Stitch a doodle

The next time you're doodling why not transform the designs into stitches? Select your scribble, copy it directly onto the fabric, and stitch away.

You will need
• Your doodles • Embroidery hoop
• Cotton or linen fabric • Embroidery threads • Sewing kit (page 112)
• Pencil

Transfer your design onto the fabric with a pencil.

NOTE: For a bag, place the hoop in the center of the fabric.

Stitch over the lines.

Stitch until the design is complete.

Remove the hoop.

How to make a bag

1 Turn the fabric over and fold it in half.

Sew the two edges together with backstitch.

2 Move the seam to the center.

Sew the bottom of the bag closed.

3 Turn the bag right side out.

4 The finished design will appear on the front.

Running stitch

Single chain stitch

Garden bird

Doodles make great buttons.

Use a running stitch to follow the outline of your doodle.

Add color to your doodles by using colored thread.

Doodle decorations

Put your doodles to work. A project that combines the whimsical and the practical, this decorated sewing case will hold your needles and threads nicely.

You will need

- 13in x 4½in (32cm x 11cm) piece felt
- 6½in x 4in (16cm x 9½cm) piece cotton fabric • Embroidery thread
- Sewing kit (page 112)
- Felt scraps for motifs

Fold the felt in half to find the center line. For the flaps, measure 2¾in (7cm) from each side. Fold in half and crease.

1

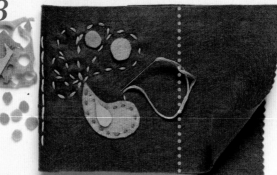

Sew the fabrics together using backstitch.

Place the cotton ········· fabric in the center of the felt.

Flap 2¾in (7cm) wide

2

Place the felt motif on the front of the case and sew it in position.

3

Build up your design with stitched outlines, such as the bird's tail.

Fill in the outlines with felt shapes and more stitches.

4

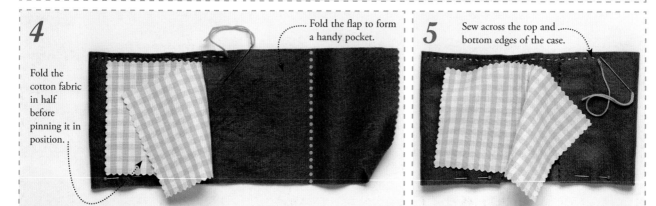

Fold the cotton fabric in half before pinning it in position.

········· Fold the flap to form a handy pocket.

5

Sew across the top and ········· bottom edges of the case.

Exotic bird design

It looks like a doodle made with pen and paper, except that this design uses fabric and thread. Begin your design with a felt shape, such as this bird, then play with the stitching, making shapes and filling in the spaces. There's no need to draw the design first— just see where inspiration takes you.

Handy pockets keep threads stored away neatly.

5

Sewing kit
and
useful know-how

Creating creatures

Every project in this book begins with a list of materials you will need. The most essential piece of equipment is the sewing kit—always have this ready. Some useful extras are also worth keeping on hand.

Sewing kit

The sewing kit essentials are featured on this page. Store them in a handy box.

Sewing thread

Keep an array of colored threads, plus some basic colors, too, such as black, gray, and brown.

Tape measure

A tape measure is a must for measuring fabric at the start of a project and for precise positioning.

Thimble

When a project calls for a lot of hand stitching, your middle finger can become sore. Wear a thimble when sewing through many pieces of fabric.

Sewing needles

Needle threader

Tapestry needles

Needles

Tapestry needles with large eyes and rounded ends work best when you're sewing with knitting yarn. Use sewing needles with large eyes and sharp ends when working with sewing or embroidery thread.

Pins

Keep straight pins on hand in one of your homemade pin cushions.

Scissors

Small, sharp embroidery scissors are useful for snipping off threads and for cutting out tiny creature shapes.

NOTE: All knitting patterns use Double Knit (DK) weight yarn

These will be useful, too...

... for everything from cutting out large pieces of fabric to stuffing toys.

Large scissors

These large scissors are ideal when you need to cut out templates or large pieces of fabric. Keep the scissors sharp, since this makes them easier to use and will also produce better results.

Pinking shears

The zigzag blade on pinking shears prevents cotton fabric from fraying when cut. The effect is attractive as well, and it can be a pretty decoration.

Embroidery thread

This extra-thick thread shows up well on projects where you want to highlight stitching. Stitches can be funtional, decorative, or both.

Felt fabric

Felt is so versatile—it's easy to shape and it doesn't fray when cut. Small scraps of felt are perfect to use for tiny projects, and they make great creature features.

Poly fill

This polyester fiber is used for all the projects in this book. It's very soft and can be easily worked into all the different animal shapes.

Buttons

Colorful buttons in all sizes work well as eyes. They can also provide added decoration to many projects.

How to stitch

The following stitches are used in projects throughout the book. They all have a different job to do when you are sewing fabric together for pillows, bags, and patchwork pieces.

How to start and finish

Begin sewing with a knot at the end of the thread. To end a row of stitches, make a tiny stitch, but do not pull it tight. Bring the thread back up through the loop and pull it tight. Do this once more in the same spot, then cut the thread.

Running stitch

This is a very versatile stitch that is used for seams, sewing fabric together, and for making gathers.

Keep the stitches and the spaces between them small and even.

Backstitch

This is a very strong stitch. It makes a continuous line of stitches so it is best for sewing two pieces of fabric securely—for instance, when you want to sew the two sides of a bag together.

Make the stitch, then bring the needle back to the place where the last stitch was finished.

Bring the needle out, ready to begin the next stitch.

VIEW FROM REVERSE

Basting stitch

This is a temporary stitch. It it is used to hold pieces of fabric in place before you sew them together properly. It is also known as a tacking stitch.

Basting stitches are like running stitches, except they are larger and don't have to be even.

Whipstitch

These tiny, neat, and even stitches are almost invisible. Use them to top sew two finished edges together, such as when sewing patchwork pieces together.

Insert the needle diagonally from the back of the fabric.

Pick up only two or three threads of fabric.

Slip stitch

Use a slip stitch when you want stitches to be invisible. This stitch is made by slipping the thread under a fold of fabric. It is often used to sew two folded edges, such as the openings of pillows.

Slide the needle into the fold of the fabric.

Bring the needle out, then slide the needle in the other side.

Lazy daisy stitch

This pretty stitch is very useful for embroidery decoration. First, use pencil to draw an outline of your daisy design on the fabric, then follow the lines with your stitches.

1 Tie a knot in your thread and pull it up through the beginning of a petal, then down at the end.

2 Bring it up through another petal until you have finished the flower.

Chain stitch

This is a very useful decorating stitch—it's great for flower stems and leaves. You may need some practice to get the stitch just right.

1 Tie a knot in the thread and pull it up through the fabric.

2 Now push the needle back down next to the thread.

3 Don't pull it tight; instead, leave a loop.

4 Bring the needle up through the loop and pull the thread through.

5 Repeat Steps 1 to 4. Keep the stitches as even as possible.

Practice chain stitch on a curved line so you can make shapes.

Blanket stitch

This stitch is good for making neat, decorative edges and for sewing one piece of fabric to another.

1 Tie a knot in the thread and pull the needle up through the fabric.

2 Push the needle back through the fabric, next to the stitch and up below it, making sure the loose end is caught, as shown.

3 Push the needle down and up again so it is the same size as the previous stitch, catching the loose thread again.

4 Repeat these steps to make more loops.

Cross-stitch

You can make whole pictures using cross-stitch.

1 Draw out crosses in light pencil on your fabric.

2 Sew a line of crosses from left to right in one direction...

... then finish them by sewing back the other way.

Stitching tip

Try to keep your stitches even and neat.

Finishing

On the back of the fabric, push the needle through the loop of the last stitch.

Pull the thread tight and repeat to make it secure.

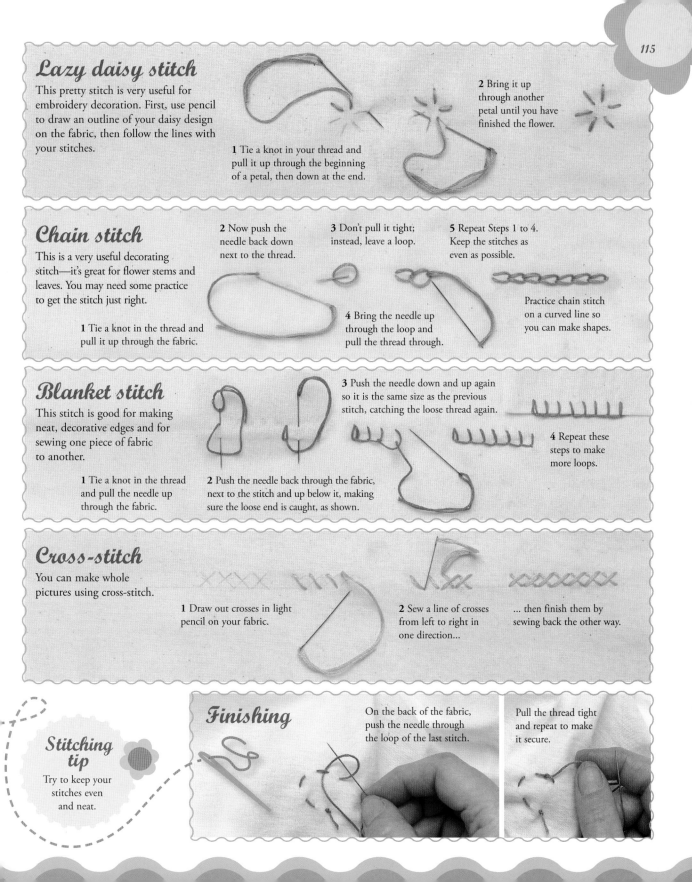

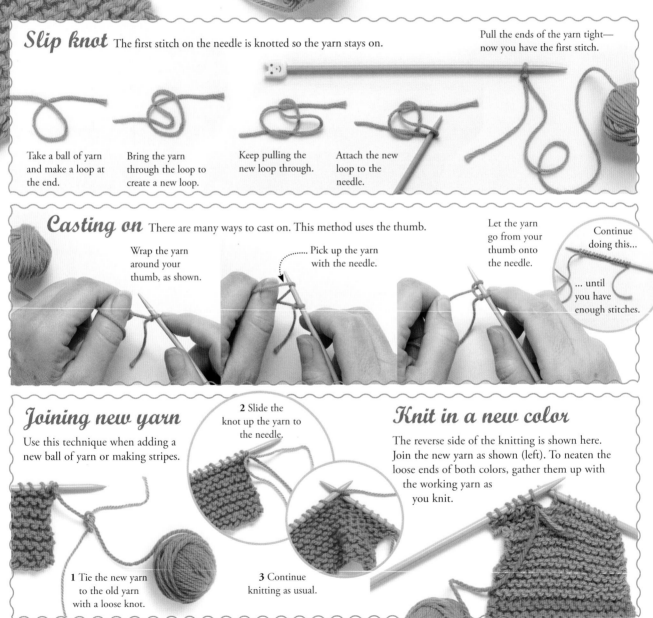

Loops, called stitches

Rows

Ball of yarn

How to knit

From casting on to casting off,
the knitting know-how you need is listed in these pages. The tips included offer a handy reference for beginners as well as more seasoned knitters.

Slip knot
The first stitch on the needle is knotted so the yarn stays on.

Pull the ends of the yarn tight—now you have the first stitch.

Take a ball of yarn and make a loop at the end.

Bring the yarn through the loop to create a new loop.

Keep pulling the new loop through.

Attach the new loop to the needle.

Casting on
There are many ways to cast on. This method uses the thumb.

Wrap the yarn around your thumb, as shown.

Pick up the yarn with the needle.

Let the yarn go from your thumb onto the needle.

Continue doing this...

... until you have enough stitches.

Joining new yarn
Use this technique when adding a new ball of yarn or making stripes.

2 Slide the knot up the yarn to the needle.

1 Tie the new yarn to the old yarn with a loose knot.

3 Continue knitting as usual.

Knit in a new color
The reverse side of the knitting is shown here. Join the new yarn as shown (left). To neaten the loose ends of both colors, gather them up with the working yarn as you knit.

Stitches 1 2 3 4 5...

How many?

The projects in this book tell you how many stitches to cast on. Lots of stitches give you a wide fabric, while few stitches make a narrow fabric.

When you are starting a new row, start with the first stitch on the right and work toward the left.

The yarn will be on the right as well.

Getting started

You will need to cast on the number of stitches required in the pattern. The stitches that are being worked will be on the left-hand needle, and the ones you have made will go on the right.

Casting off

1 Begin the row by knitting two stitches.

2 Pick up the first stitch with the left needle.

3 Carry this first stitch over the second stitch and over the end of the needle.

4 Repeat steps 1 through 3...

5 ... until one stitch remains. Open up the loop.

6 Cut the yarn and place the end in the loop.

7 Pull the yarn to close the loop.

Neaten the ends

Sew in ends when adding new yarn or neaten the loose ends of finished pieces.

Use this method to neaten seams and when knitting stripes.

Use this method when neatening loose ends of finished pieces.

Thread the end with a tapestry needle.

Sew the thread into the edge of the knitting.

Bring the needle out and cut the yarn.

Thread the needle onto the loose end and sew down the side of the knitting.

Bring the needle out and cut the yarn.

Knit stitch

Also called plain stitch, knit stitch is the most widely used stitch. It's simple to make and is used in many projects in this book. Just ask Ted!

Method 1

1 Hold the knitting with your hands in this position.

Take the yarn around the back.

Place the needle in the back of the stitch.

2 Wrap the yarn under and around the needle from right to left.

Method 2 This method is often preferred by left-handers.

1 Place the yarn between the fingers of your left hand.

2 Use your index finger to move the yarn.

Place the needle into the stitch from the back.

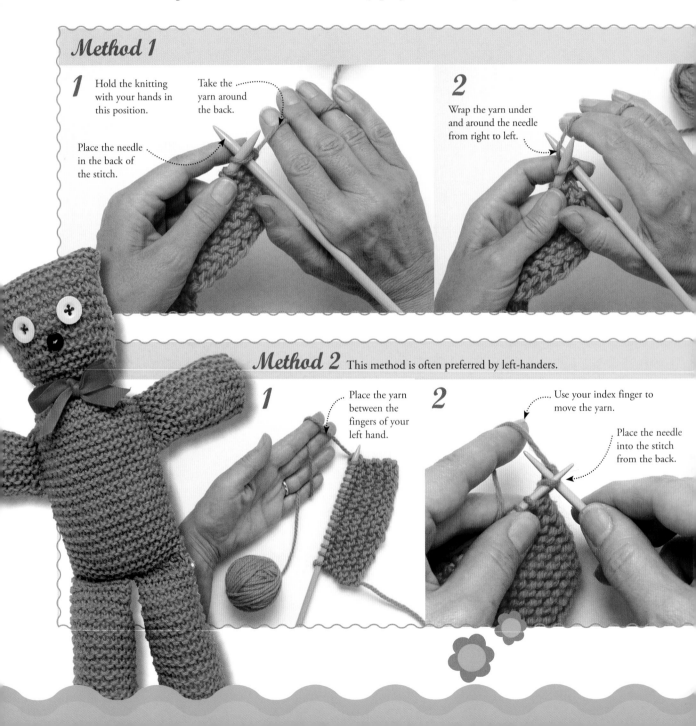

Garter stitch

Garter stitch is
also made if you
knit every row in
purl stitch.

Garter stitch isn't an actual stitch; instead,
it's the name given to a piece of knitting
where every row is knitted in knit stitch.
The effect is bumpy on both sides.

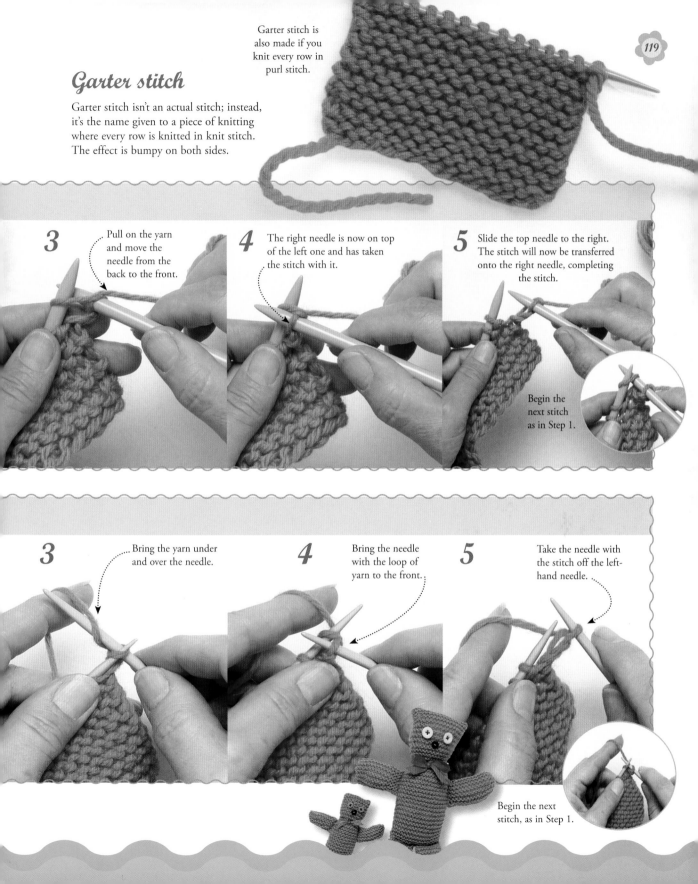

3 Pull on the yarn
and move the
needle from the
back to the front.

4 The right needle is now on top
of the left one and has taken
the stitch with it.

5 Slide the top needle to the right.
The stitch will now be transferred
onto the right needle, completing
the stitch.

Begin the
next stitch
as in Step 1.

3 Bring the yarn under
and over the needle.

4 Bring the needle
with the loop of
yarn to the front.

5 Take the needle with
the stitch off the left-
hand needle.

Begin the next
stitch, as in Step 1.

For purl stitch, the needle goes in the front of the stitch.

The yarn is also to the front.

Purl stitch

Working from the front, make this stitch by placing the needle in front of the stitch. When knit and purl stitch rows are alternated, the knitting looks smooth. Check the knittens to see the results.

Method 1

1 Hold the knitting with your hands in this position.

Bring the yarn to the front.

Place the needle in the front of the stitch.

2 Take the yarn between the needles.

3 Wrap it around the needle from right to left.

Method 2   This method is often preferred by left-handers.

1 Place the right-hand needle in the front of the stitch.

Hold the needle in your left hand with the yarn at the front of the work.

2 Wind the yarn around the front of the needle.

3 Wind the yarn around again.

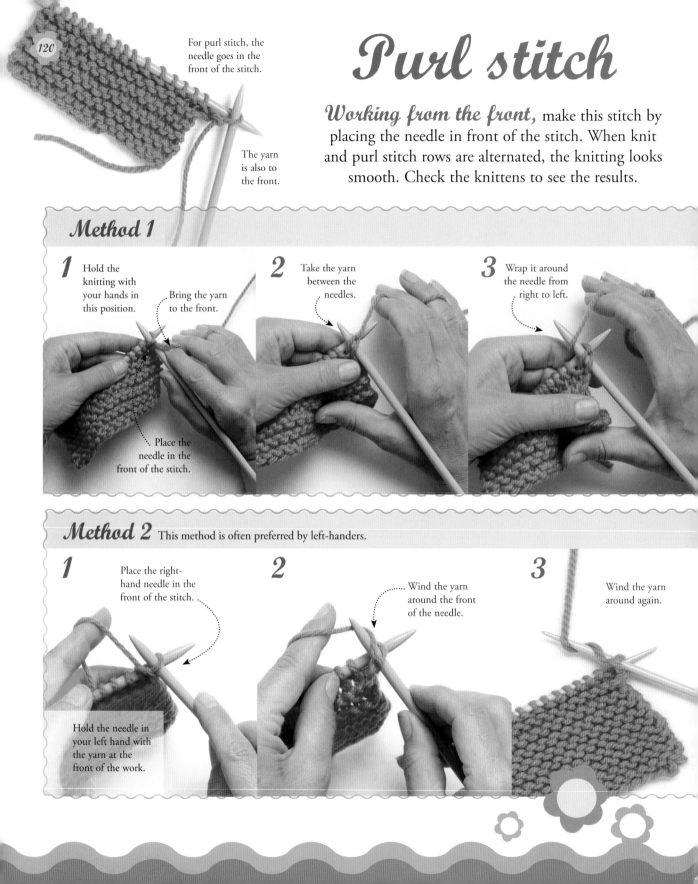

Purl stitch + knit stitch = stockinette stitch

Stockinette stitch isn't an actual stitch at all. Instead, it is made by working a knit row, then a purl row, a knit row, then a purl row, and so on. The result is a smooth front to the knitting and a "knobby" back.

FRONT
The knit-stitch side

BACK
The purl-stitch side

4 Pull on the yarn and move the needle from front to back...

5 ... taking the stitch with it.

6 Take the rest of the yarn off the needle to complete the stitch.

Begin the next stitch, as in Step 1.

4 Bring the right-hand needle from front to back, taking the yarn with it.

5 Pull the rest of the stitch off the needle.

6 Now you are ready to begin the next stitch, starting at step 1 again.

Knitting shapes

INCREASE SHAPE

An extra stitch has been made at the beginning and the end of each row.

Two stitches have been knitted together at the beginning and end of each row.

DECREASE SHAPE

You can shape the knitting by adding (increasing) or taking away (decreasing) stitches. There are many different ways to do this, but here are two simple methods that work well.

Make a stitch: Increasing

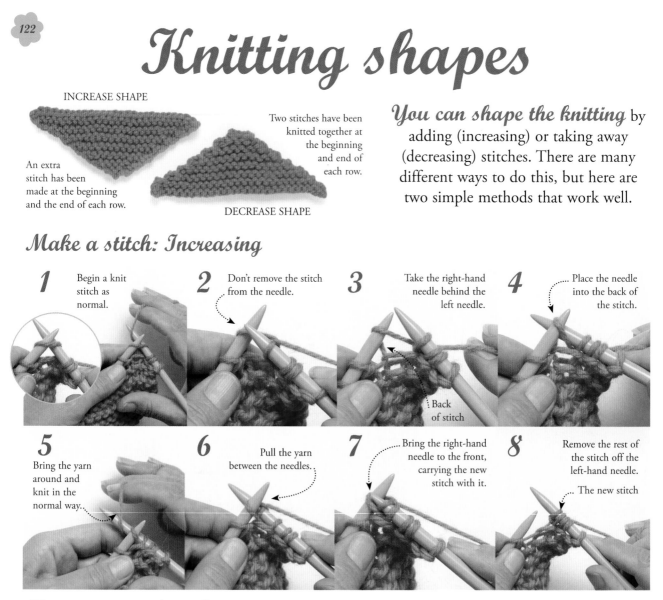

1 Begin a knit stitch as normal.

2 Don't remove the stitch from the needle.

3 Take the right-hand needle behind the left needle.

Back of stitch

4 Place the needle into the back of the stitch.

5 Bring the yarn around and knit in the normal way.

6 Pull the yarn between the needles.

7 Bring the right-hand needle to the front, carrying the new stitch with it.

8 Remove the rest of the stitch off the left-hand needle.

The new stitch

Knit two together: Decreasing

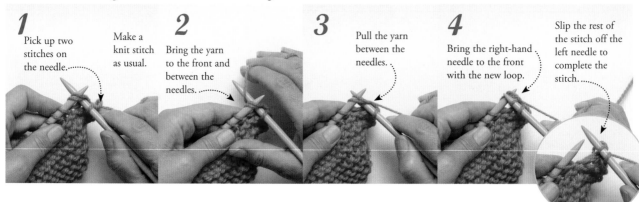

1 Pick up two stitches on the needle.

Make a knit stitch as usual.

2 Bring the yarn to the front and between the needles.

3 Pull the yarn between the needles.

4 Bring the right-hand needle to the front with the new loop.

Slip the rest of the stitch off the left needle to complete the stitch.

Threading needles

NEEDLE TYPES

Tapestry needle | Sewing needle

Large eye, rounded end | Small eye, sharp end

THREADING EMBROIDERY THREAD OR WOOL YARN

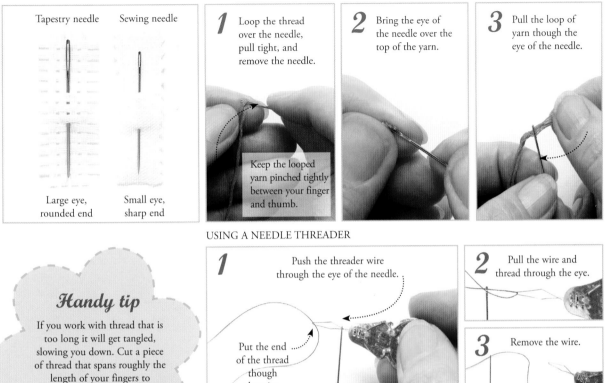

1 Loop the thread over the needle, pull tight, and remove the needle.

Keep the looped yarn pinched tightly between your finger and thumb.

2 Bring the eye of the needle over the top of the yarn.

3 Pull the loop of yarn though the eye of the needle.

USING A NEEDLE THREADER

1 Push the threader wire through the eye of the needle.

Put the end of the thread though the wire.

2 Pull the wire and thread through the eye.

3 Remove the wire.

Handy tip

If you work with thread that is too long it will get tangled, slowing you down. Cut a piece of thread that spans roughly the length of your fingers to your elbow.

Sewing on a button

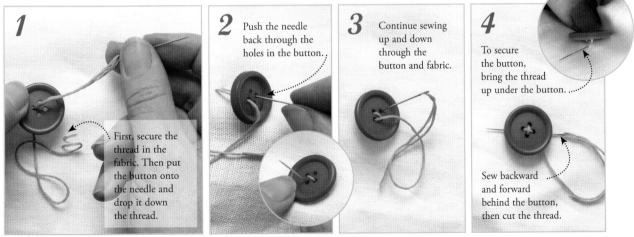

1 First, secure the thread in the fabric. Then put the button onto the needle and drop it down the thread.

2 Push the needle back through the holes in the button.

3 Continue sewing up and down through the button and fabric.

4 To secure the button, bring the thread up under the button.

Sew backward and forward behind the button, then cut the thread.

Index

126